At Issue

| Hurricane Katrina

Other Books in the At Issue Series:

At Issue

Hurricane Katrina

Diane Andrews Henningfeld, Book Editor

GREENHAVEN PRESS
A part of Gale, Cengage Learning

GALE
CENGAGE Learning™

Detroit • New York • San Francisco • New Haven, Conn • Waterville, Maine • London

GALE
CENGAGE Learning

Christine Nasso, *Publisher*
Elizabeth Des Chenes, *Managing Editor*

© 2010 Greenhaven Press, a part of Gale, Cengage Learning.

Gale and Greenhaven Press are registered trademarks used herein under license.

For more information, contact:
Greenhaven Press
27500 Drake Rd.
Farmington Hills, MI 48331-3535
Or you can visit our Internet site at gale.cengage.com

For product information and technology assistance, contact us at

Gale Customer Support, 1-800-877-4253
For permission to use material from this text or product, submit all requests online at www.cengage.com/permissions

Further permissions questions can be e-mailed to permissionrequest@cengage.com

Articles in Greenhaven Press anthologies are often edited for length to meet page requirements. In addition, original titles of these works are changed to clearly present the main thesis and to explicitly indicate the author's opinion. Every effort is made to ensure that Greenhaven Press accurately reflects the original intent of the authors. Every effort has been made to trace the owners of copyrighted material.

Cover photograph © Sue Poynton. Image from BigStockPhoto.com.

LIBRARY OF CONGRESS CATALOGING-IN-PUBLICATION DATA

Hurricane Katrina / Diane Andrews Henningfeld, book editor.
    p. cm. -- (At issue)
    Includes bibliographical references and index.
    ISBN 978-0-7377-4882-6 (hardcover) -- ISBN 978-0-7377-4883-3 (pbk.)
    1. Hurricane Katrina, 2005--Juvenile literature. 2. Hurricanes--Juvenile literature. 3. Disaster relief--United States--Juvenile literature. 4. Rescue work--United States--Juvenile literature. I. Henningfeld, Diane Andrews.
    HV636 2005 .U6 H865 2008
    976'.044--dc22
                                      2010003359

Printed in the United States of America
1 2 3 4 5 6 7 14 13 12 11 10

Contents

Introduction

When Hurricane Katrina slammed into the Gulf of Mexico coastlines of Mississippi and Louisiana, bringing with it winds of more than 120 miles per hour and a storm surge of thirty feet, the destruction was immense. Many died, and many more lost their homes, businesses, and ways of life. It was in the period *after* the storm, however, that the greatest damage was done: When the levee system of New Orleans catastrophically failed, flood waters rushed in, covering more than 80 percent of the city.

Although many residents had evacuated the area in anticipation of the storm, many others remained trapped in New Orleans by poverty, illness, or old age, unable to find a means out of the city. In the days and weeks that followed Katrina's rough visit, emergency personnel worked tirelessly to pluck trapped residents from rooftops, provide water and food to those in need, and offer medical assistance where necessary. In spite of this, sources agree that more than eighteen hundred people died directly or indirectly from the storm, and more than seven hundred remained missing a year later. Some of the dead were victims of dehydration; others died from drowning, injuries sustained during the flood, or a lack of basic medical care.

Still others died through violence, as armed security guards, police, and even vigilante groups shot those they thought were looting or stealing. Many of those killed in this way were African Americans who were guilty only of being in the wrong place at the wrong time. Part of the problem was one of perception. Was a woman who tried to find food for her children in a time of crisis a good mother or a looter? Was a man out looking for his son a grieving father or a potential troublemaker? Sometimes people quickly leapt to judgment based on unspoken and unconscious assumptions. For example, according to Rebecca Solnit in the *Guardian* on August 26, 2009, Donnell Herrington stayed in New Orleans to care for his grandparents. After rescuing many people by boat, Herrington attempted to leave himself, only to be shot twice by white vigilantes trying to prevent him from crossing a bridge into the community of Algiers. Solnit writes, "The vigilantes shot him because he was black, and because they could get away with it, and because they were inflamed by the news accounts."

According to the 2000 U.S. census, 67 percent of the population of New Orleans was African American, and nearly 30 percent of the population of New Orleans lived at or below the poverty level in that year. Perhaps not coincidentally the areas of the city most affected by the wrath of Katrina and its aftermath were largely poor, African American neighborhoods such as the Ninth Ward. Indeed, many survivors and historians of Hurricane Katrina believe that much of the suffering and terror inflicted on the residents of New Orleans was not only from the fury of the storm, but also from an inadequate governmental response, fueled by institutional racism and disregard for the poor.

An August 20, 2006, Associated Press (AP) article, for example, reported that Ray Nagin, mayor of New Orleans, "blamed racism and government bureaucracy for hamstringing his city's ability to weather Hurricane Katrina and recover from the disaster." Speaking to the National Association of Black Journalists, Nagin stated, "And I, to this day, believe that if that would have happened in Orange County, California, if that would have happened in South Beach, Miami, it would have been a different response."

Nagin is not alone in his belief. Craig Palosky and Rakesh Singh, reporting on a 2007 Kaiser Family Foundation house-to-house survey they conducted, wrote that "the survey . . . found a sharp divide in the way that African Americans and whites in the New Orleans area experienced the storm and perceive the recovery efforts." According to the survey, "twice as many African Americans as whites in Orleans (59 percent vs. 29 percent) reported that their lives were still 'very' or 'somewhat' disrupted." The divide is even greater in the perception of the recovery effort in the city: "More than half (55 percent) of blacks in the parish said they face worse treatment and opportunities than whites as part of the rebuilding process; among white Orleans residents, only 19 percent said blacks are being treated worse."

Not everyone believes that racism had anything to do with the terrible suffering inflicted on thousands of New Orleans' poorest residents, however. On January 29, 2009, former secretary of state Condoleezza Rice appeared on the ABC television show *The View* to talk about her experiences in the George W. Bush administration. When asked about the federal response to Katrina, Rice replied that the storm was the "worst natural disaster" experienced by the United States. She went on to say,

> What really did make me angry was the implication that some people made that somehow President Bush allowed this to happen because these people were black. And for somebody to say that about the president of the United States, a president of the United States who I know well and a president of the United States who is my friend, I was appalled.

Some also see the tragedy of Katrina as rooted in issues of class and poverty rather than race. Jennifer Mascia, writing in the *New York Times* on November 22, 2009, reports on one survivor of Katrina, Jennifer Hero, who is now living in Brooklyn, New York. "Her displacement," Mascia writes, "followed by her struggle to get back on her feet in the four years since, has given her a unique perspective on poverty in America. . . . She contends that the errors committed by government at local, state, and federal levels after the storm exposed not deepseated racism, but classism."

Hurricane Katrina was far more than a storm. It was a disaster of near-apocalyptic scale for those who experienced it. The controversies surrounding both the preparation for the storm, the governmental response, and the ongoing suffering of those whose lives were torn apart by Katrina are likely to rage for decades to come. The viewpoints that follow explore some of these issues.

1

Americans Are Now More Able to Help At-Risk Populations After Disasters

Timothy Manning

Timothy Manning is the deputy administrator of the Federal Emergency Management Agency (FEMA). FEMA is part of the U.S. Department of Homeland Security and is tasked with disaster mitigation, preparedness, and response and recovery planning.

Hurricane Katrina taught several important lessons including the need to identify those populations that are most vulnerable to injury and death during such a storm. Since Katrina, the Federal Emergency Management Agency (FEMA) has initiated many activities that will help at-risk populations in an emergency, including the establishment of the Citizen Corps, a grassroots project that involves all the members of a community in preparedness and training. In addition, the agency has helped local governments with disaster planning and training, benefiting all citizens and improving hurricane preparedness. Through a combination of government intervention and personal preparedness, Americans are now able to cope with natural disasters.

Throughout the history of emergency management planning, considerations for special needs populations have been inadequate. From the 1930s, when disaster response was ad hoc and largely focused on the repair of damaged infra-

Timothy Manning, "Emergency Preparedness, Aging and Special Needs," Hearing before the Special Committee on Aging, United States Senate, June 24, 2009. www.aging.senate .gov.

structure, through the present day, special needs populations were often given insufficient consideration. This fact was evident in 2003 during the California wildfires, and when Hurricane Katrina devastated the Gulf Coast in 2005. During these events, a substantial number of individuals with special needs did not receive appropriate warning, were unable to access shelters, went without medical intervention or, at worst, perished. During the 2006 Nationwide Plan Review, a sample of emergency management plans from various regions in the United States was reviewed by subject-matter experts on disability and aging. The review confirmed that many of the 2006 emergency plans overlooked these populations. The review concluded that "substantial improvement is necessary to integrate people with disabilities in emergency planning and readiness."

Assisting Vulnerable Populations in an Emergency

Numerous "lessons learned" reports that followed Hurricane Katrina also identified a large segment of the U.S. population that may not be able to successfully plan for and respond to an emergency with resources typically accessible to the general population. The current general population is one that is diverse, aging, and focused on maintaining independence as long as possible. The popularity of living situations that provide an "as needed" level of care in the least restrictive manner is fast becoming the norm. Consideration must therefore be given to people who may be able to function independently under normal situations, but who may need assistance in an emergency situation.

For example, in the event of a disaster, it is estimated that about 13 million individuals age 50 or older in the United States would need evacuation assistance, and about half of these individuals will require such assistance from someone outside of their household. There are well over one million people in the United States receiving home health care according to 2000 data cited by the National Center for Health Care Statistics. Populations such as these must be considered when emergency plans are developed to accurately assess the resources needed to adequately respond when a disaster strikes. The 2000 census reported that 18 percent of those surveyed speak a language other than English at home. This statistic highlights the need to ensure the effectiveness of emergency communications. All of these examples serve to demonstrate that community emergency planning must go beyond traditional considerations.

FEMA [Federal Emergency Management Agency] is working hard to ensure that its own basic planning addresses special needs populations and that we are supporting and assisting states, tribes and localities in this regard. We are also reinforcing the critical and enduring need for personal preparedness, to encourage individuals to adequately prepare themselves for disaster events, recognizing that better individual preparedness translates into better community preparedness and resilience.

Specific Plans to Help the Elderly and Disabled in a Disaster

FEMA is directly engaged in activities that will address special needs populations, including the elderly. In coordination with FEMA's Office of Equal Rights, DHS [Department of Homeland Security] Office for Civil Rights and Civil Liberties, and the National Advisory Council, as well as state, tribal, and local disability and special need agencies, the FEMA Disability Coordinator has built a viable network to ensure that the needs of the elderly and persons with disabilities are addressed during and following disasters. For example, FEMA:

- Developed a FEMA handbook called *Accommodating People with Disabilities and Special Needs in a Disaster*, to assist FEMA, state emergency managers, FEMA partners, and other stakeholders in accommodating people with disabilities and special needs in a disaster.

- Developed go-kits to be distributed to all the regions to assist states with the evacuation and sheltering needs of special needs and disability populations in a catastrophic event. These go-kits are designed for people who experience hearing impairment, visual disabilities, cognitive disabilities, or mobility disabilities, as well as for children and people with service animals.

- Developed with Mass Care [a division within FEMA] a functional need support plan to share with the states to ensure that people with disabilities and other special needs are provided the accommodations in a shelter to ensure inclusion and independence.

- Developed plans for working with the disaster recovery centers to ensure that the centers are accessible to everyone and are adequately staffed with interpreters.

- Collaborates with local disability and other special needs agencies in the field before and during all disasters, ensuring that the agencies are communicating with first responders, shelter managers, and impacted special needs populations to identify and address any gaps.

- Provides training and resources for emergency managers on how to develop and include plans to accommodate evacuation and sheltering concerns for people with disabilities and other special needs.

- Collaborates with federal and state exercise planners to ensure that the exercises include evacuation and sheltering methods for people with different types of disabilities and other special needs, and engage persons with disabilities and other special needs as participants in the development and execution of exercises.

- Works through FEMA Public Affairs to ensure that all materials are in alternative formats, that materials are 508 [a section of the Rehabilitation Act] compliant, and that interpreters are available.

- Develops disability and special needs subject matter teams to work with states during a disaster in order to ensure accommodation for people with disabilities and other special needs.

Citizen Corps: A Grassroots Initiative

Citizen Corps is FEMA's grassroots initiative to actively involve all citizens in the security of their communities through planning, personal preparedness, training, and volunteer service. The Citizen Corps's mission is based on the principle that full citizen engagement—including active participation by citizens with disabilities, children and the elderly—is of critical importance at all levels and in all areas of all-hazard emergency preparedness, planning, mitigation, response and recovery. As part of FEMA's Community Preparedness Division, Citizen Corps will work closely with FEMA's National Disability Coordinator.

Emergency management takes into consideration planning for the safety of every person in the community during and following a disaster.

Promoting active participation by organizations and individuals representing persons with disabilities is an important part of the mission for the 2,100 councils at the state, local, and tribal levels who implement Citizen Corps. Working with local Citizen Corps councils, representatives from the disability community are helping to strengthen community preparedness by developing emergency operations plans that address accessibility and inclusion in all aspects of planning, ranging from alert and warning systems to evacuation and shelter plans. Collaborative community efforts support campaigns for outreach, disaster preparedness education, and 72-hour kits for citizens who need assistance. Partner programs like Community Emergency Response Teams (CERT) provide all-ability training for community volunteers.

At the national level, Citizen Corps promotes inclusion and a focus on the disability and special needs community by integrating these priorities into Homeland Security policies. Citizen Corps actively seeks and publicizes, through newsletters and other forums, examples of how state and local councils and programs collaborate with organizations to strengthen community preparedness related to these needs.

FEMA Assists with Disaster Planning

Emergency management takes into consideration planning for the safety of every person in the community during and following a disaster. Taking into consideration populations historically considered "vulnerable," "at-risk," or "special needs" ultimately improves the overall community's post-disaster sustainability. In addition to active program support, FEMA assists states and localities with planning guidance for state and local preparedness efforts.

FEMA will shortly issue guidelines on special needs populations through its Comprehensive Preparedness Guide 301: *Emergency Management Planning Guide for Special Needs Populations.* This guide, developed in collaboration with DHS Office for Civil Rights and Civil Liberties, is currently available to all of our nation's communities as an interim document on the FEMA Web site. It addresses many of the issues that will confront us in providing care to elderly and other special needs populations in the face of disaster, as well as the importance of personal preparedness.

FEMA Prioritizes Training

Training development and delivery for special needs populations and citizen preparedness have been and will continue to be FEMA priorities. The Department [of Homeland Security] has supported the development of a variety of course curricula, including:

- Emergency Responders and the Deaf and Hard of Hearing Community: Taking the First Steps to Disaster Preparedness

This course addresses fundamentals associated with emergency preparedness and response as it relates to deaf, hard of hearing, late-deafened, and deaf-blind individuals and fosters a greater understanding between this community and the emergency responders that serve them.

- Responding to the Unique Evacuation and Shelter-in-Place Needs of Medically Dependent People During a Disaster Situation

FEMA is partnering with and supporting the Yale New Haven Health System in the development of a training program that will equip local and regional emergency planners and responders with homeland security–related responsibilities to address the unique evacuation and shelter-in-place requirements of medically dependent persons residing in high-occupancy facilities, including hospitals, nursing homes and assisted-living facilities. Course content will focus on pre-event preparation, tactical operations for evacuation and sheltering-in-place during a disaster and strategies for returning individuals to their place of residence at the conclusion of the disaster. Approximately 2,000 individuals will be trained via the instructor-led course and 33,000 in the online course. We expect this course curriculum to be available in early 2010.

Specific Training Opportunities

Additionally, our Emergency Management Institute provides a variety of training opportunities, including:

- *Emergency Planning and Special Needs Populations field course*—This 2-1/2 day course is intended to provide those with responsibilities for providing emergency planning or care for seniors, people with disabilities, and/or special needs groups with the skills and knowledge they will need to prepare for, respond to, and recover from emergency situations. The target audience includes emergency managers, senior first response personnel, special needs coordinators, human services organization personnel, facility planners, community-based organizational personnel, advocacy group personnel, elected officials, public health personnel, and National Voluntary Organizations Active in Disaster (National VOAD) personnel.

- *Special Needs Planning Considerations for Emergency Management independent study course*—This course is designed for emergency management and first responder personnel to enable them to better understand the special needs population and teach how to partner with persons with special needs as well as their support providers and organizations.

- *Special Needs Planning Considerations for Service and Support Providers independent study course*—This course is designed for people who work with the elderly and people with disabilities, and will teach how to partner with local emergency management to better prepare for all phases of an emergency.

These are just a few examples of the kinds of specialized training that FEMA and the Department [of Homeland Security] are making available nationally.

Disaster Simulations

Congress included, within the Post-Katrina Emergency Management Reform Act of 2006, a requirement that our National Exercise Program "shall be designed to provide systematic evaluation of readiness; and designed to address the unique requirements of populations with special needs."

In times of crisis, government plays a critical role in coordinating response and recovery efforts, especially in protecting and providing for our most vulnerable populations.

To address this requirement, National Exercise Program Tier I and Tier II exercises, including the TOPOFF 4 Full-Scale Exercise, have included special needs-focused objectives. Specifically, one of the objectives for TOPOFF 4 was to examine the handling of mental health and special needs issues arising during and after a radiological dispersal device event that was at the center of the exercise scenario. This "special needs population" element was identified as a strength in the overall exercise design and has been incorporated in future National Level Exercises planning.

[DHS] Secretary [Janet] Napolitano, FEMA Administrator [W. Craig] Fugate and I are committed to advancing our nation's preparedness. Our efforts must begin with personal preparedness—a process of individual thinking and consideration of basic steps that each of us must take to help prevent and prepare for the next disaster. All Americans must take responsibility for preparing themselves, their families and their communities for the next disaster. In times of crisis, government plays a critical role in coordinating response and recovery efforts, especially in protecting and providing for our most vulnerable populations. Improved personal preparedness will increase the government's capacity to ensure the safety and well-being of the American public. Communicating the importance of preparedness is a cornerstone of our strategy moving forward, and with the continued support of Congress, we believe that considerable progress is within reach.

2

Americans Remain Unprepared for a Major Hurricane

PR Newswire

PR Newswire delivers news and multimedia content to investors, media, and consumers.

A survey conducted by The Ampersand Agency on behalf of CPL Retail Energy reveals that more than 60 percent of Texas Gulf Coast residents do not believe they are prepared for a major hurricane. The survey reveals that only a quarter of the residents had an accessible first-aid kit and three days' supply of food.

Despite the impacts of [Hurricanes] Ike, Dolly, Edouard and Gustav a few short months ago, a new survey conducted on behalf of CPL Retail Energy suggests that Texans could do more to get ready for hurricane season.

More than 60 percent of Texas Gulf Coast residents do not believe themselves to be well prepared for the next hurricane, and of those who do consider themselves to be moderately or well prepared, few have taken the necessary pre- and post-hurricane steps to be ready for hurricane season. This news comes just in time for Hurricane Preparedness Week, beginning May 24 [2009].

"We conducted the survey to assess current levels, attitudes and opinions of hurricane preparedness among Texas Gulf Coast residents to ensure they know how to safeguard their families and homes," said Lisa Dornan, director of public relations for CPL. Dornan emphasizes the importance of the survey as hurricane season's official June 1 start approaches.

Of immediate pre-hurricane precautions, only about a third of respondents had a written family disaster plan. Fewer than half of those heads of household who consider themselves very well prepared say they have one, and less than a quarter of the moderately prepared or ill-prepared families have one. Although most have taken some precautions, like having a vehicle in good repair with a full tank of gas and ensuring that important household papers, like school records, house title and insurance records are in one place, Gulf Coast residents need the most education about home preparations—including unplugging major electrical appliances and turning off the water to their home.

Only a quarter of residents had three days of nonperishable food or a first-aid kit on hand, and only one in five had sufficient water stored for an emergency.

"We found that more than 60 percent of Texas coastal residents do not unplug their washer and dryer to prevent power-surge damage or turn off their water to prevent flooding from broken pipes. In addition, about 88 percent do not remove fuses from their air conditioning systems to prevent damage," said Dornan.

Many Unprepared

In post-hurricane preparations, survey results show that overall, only a quarter of residents had three days of nonperishable food or a first-aid kit on hand, and only one in five had sufficient water stored for an emergency. Only a quarter of those over the age of 65 have a two-week supply of prescription medications in case of an emergency. Of the 11.5 percent who have an adult who will need special assistance beyond a family member to evacuate, more than 70 percent are not registered with 2-1-1 Special Needs Registry.

The survey also questioned residents on individual evacuation procedures. Only one in four residents said they would leave immediately during a voluntary evacuation. Seven out of 10 say they would leave immediately in case of a mandatory evacuation, leaving over a quarter waiting to see what the storm does or staying for the duration. Of those who would stay for the duration of the storm, residents were either those who considered themselves to be well prepared or least prepared.

"Our experience has shown that the bigger the storm, the more damage to transmission lines, which will leave residents without power for extended periods; even those who evacuate are likely to come back before power has been restored and we want to make sure they are prepared," said Dornan. "The most important message to those who reside in zones which are advised to 'hunker down' for the storm or residents who make the decision to stay for the duration of a storm is to ensure you have the appropriate amount of critical supplies such as water, batteries, nonperishable food items and prescription drugs. Regardless of whether you stay or leave, it is important to unplug appliances and electronics along with removing A/C [air conditioning] fuses to avoid damage caused by power surges when lines and power are restored."

Tips for Preparation

As a major energy provider to the Gulf Coast area, CPL Retail Energy wants to ensure that Texas customers know how to safeguard their families and homes. CPL is providing useful tips in helping prepare for a hurricane and avoiding electrical issues during the aftermath:

Before a Hurricane

- Stock nonperishable food supplies, a first-aid kit, a battery-powered radio, flashlights, and extra batteries in airtight containers.

- Adjust refrigerator temperatures to the coldest settings to reduce the potential for food spoiling if the power is temporarily lost.

- Have a nonelectric analog telephone or a fully charged cell phone available in case you need to make an emergency call during a power outage.

- Heed the advice of local authorities. Evacuate if ordered.

- If an evacuation is necessary, unplug all appliances, TVs and computers before leaving your home.

- Remove fuses from air conditioning system to prevent damage.

- Turn off water to prevent flooding from broken pipes.

- Turn off gas to prevent leaks from occurring.

During a Hurricane

- Turn off electricity at the main circuit breaker or fuse box to protect appliances from power surges.

- Do not take a bath or shower and avoid water faucets, which can conduct electricity.

- Do not handle any electrical equipment and do not use the telephone except for an emergency.

After a Hurricane

- When power is restored to your home, do not start all major appliances at once; turn them on gradually to reduce damage to sensitive equipment.

- Avoid downed, damaged or loose power lines and report them immediately to the local police and fire department as well as to the local transmission and distribution services provider in your area.

- Never use a generator indoors, including garages, basements and crawl spaces, even with ventilation. Exhaust fumes contain high levels of carbon monoxide which can be deadly if inhaled. Even when left outside, keep generators away from doors and windows, and at least 10 feet away from your home. Also, allow your generator to cool off before refilling it with gas—splashing gas on hot generator components can lead to fire.

- Do not use electrical or gas appliances that have been wet, and do not turn on damaged appliances because of the hazards of electric shock or fire.

- Never use charcoal indoors because burning charcoal produces high levels of carbon monoxide that can reach lethal levels in enclosed spaces.

Only one in four residents said they would leave immediately during a voluntary evacuation.

The Survey and CPL Retail Energy

The Texas Gulf Coast Hurricane Preparedness Survey conducted by The Ampersand Agency on behalf of CPL Retail Energy was conducted in two stages with a four-zone breakdown of the region: Harris County, East, Southwest and Nueces/Cameron Counties. From April 15–22, 331 Texas Gulf Coast heads of household, aged 18 and over, were sampled with a plus or minus 5.5 percent margin of error. From April 23–26, additional people were surveyed, bringing the sample up to 99 people in Cameron and 101 people in Nueces County. Those samples were then weighted down. This oversampling allowed CPL to analyze the result in each of those two counties with a 10 percent margin of error, giving an increase in the reliability of the survey.

CPL Retail Energy is part of the Centrica group of companies, one of the largest multistate providers of retail energy services in North America. The North American operations have grown to more than 5 million residential and commercial customer relationships. Through its Direct Energy, CPL Retail Energy and WTU Retail Energy brands, the company is the third largest retail energy provider in Texas, and owns a series of energy-related services companies. The company also offers comprehensive energy solutions to more than 60,000 businesses across North America. Globally, the Centrica group of companies is a leading provider of energy and other essential services with approximately 32 million customer relationships. For more information, visit http://www.cplretailenergy.com/.

Texas Gulf Coast Fact Sheet— Hurricane Preparedness

In addition to securing your home [and] gathering important documents and emergency supplies, some less common preparations can be taken now:

- Over 70% surveyed do not have a written family disaster plan

- 15% of ages 18–34 and 23% [of] African American respondents do not have a vehicle in good repair with a full tank of gas

- 25% of the general population including seniors and Hispanics, as well as 45% of African Americans surveyed do not have hurricane insurance coverage

Of those surveyed, most respondents unplug TVs and computers and remove items from their yards or patios, however, there are additional home preparations:

- More than 40% of those surveyed do not secure their homes by boarding up or installing shutters. African Americans total more than 68%

- 60% of those surveyed do not unplug the washer and dryer to prevent power-surge damage

- Over 60% do not turn off water services to prevent flooding from broken pipes

- Over 85% do not remove fuses from air conditioning system to prevent damage

Of those surveyed, an average of 75% of the respondents have a post-storm emergency kit, but the majority were lacking in the quantity of needed supplies:

- Over 65% do not have a three-day supply of nonperishable foods

- More than 80% of respondents do not have a fully stocked first-aid kit

- Over 70% do not have a two-week supply of prescription drugs. 90% of ages 18–34 lack the needed supply of prescription drugs

- Greater than 60% of those surveyed do not have one gallon of drinking water per person per day to last for one week

- 80% do not have an emergency cash supply

30–50% of the Texas Gulf Coast general population will not leave until a mandatory evacuation is ordered

16% of seniors and minorities on the Texas Gulf Coast will stay for the duration of a storm regardless of a mandatory evacuation order

15–25% of minorities on the Texas Gulf Coast need evacuation assistance beyond family or friends, yet more than 50% of those are not registered with 2-1-1 Special Needs Registry

3

New Orleans Is Being Made Safe from Hurricanes

Susan Spaht

Susan Spaht writes for the Task Force Hope Status Report Newsletter *of the U.S. Army Corps of Engineers.*

The U.S. Army Corps of Engineers is building the Hurricane and Storm Damage Risk Reduction System (HSDRRS) in New Orleans to provide protection from storm surges likely to occur only once in a century. The target date for completion is June 2011. The project is a collaborative effort among the Corps, the state of Louisiana, levee authorities, and local governments. In some places, the Corps has had to resort to interim strategies to provide 100-year level protection while more permanent solutions are being formulated. The project comprises floodgates, surge barriers, pumping stations, and improved canal closures. The Corps believes that the system's success in protecting New Orleans from Hurricanes Gustav and Ike in 2008 is a strong measure of its effectiveness.

"We set a goal of having 100-year level surge protection in place for the greater New Orleans area by June 2011, and that is what we continue to work toward," said Karen Durham-Aguilera, director of Task Force Hope. "It is a goal that is ambitious and aggressive, but achievable.

"All along, we said we cannot achieve this monumental effort alone—it will require continued shared responsibilities, organizational teamwork and constant effort by the [U.S. Army] Corps of Engineers, the state of Louisiana, the levee authorities, the parishes, other federal agencies, all of our partners."

The [U.S. Army] Corps of Engineers [hereinafter the Corps] is constructing a nearly $15 billion program—the Hurricane and Storm Damage Risk Reduction System (HSDRRS)—in a mere six years. It is an unprecedented and enormous effort that involves development of new design criteria, project modeling, environmental compliance including more than 125 public meetings, and acquiring private and government-owned real estate. Additionally, the Corps is responsible for construction of interior drainage projects under the Southeast Louisiana Urban Flood Damage Reduction Project (SELA), and other auxiliary features authorized and funded by Congress.

A Cooperative Effort

The Corps is responsible for design, plans, specifications and construction of HSDRRS projects, and meeting important milestones with its partners to assure its June 2011 goal. "These are milestones that must happen to get to the goal of 2011," said the director.

The state of Louisiana, in addition to its cost-share commitment, is responsible for acquiring the necessary real estate interests, coordinating utility relocations where necessary, and issuing rights of entry for construction of HSDRRS projects.

For every project, whether cost-shared or fully federally funded, the Corps must have a written Project Partnership Agreement (PPA), a document that defines roles, responsibilities and obligations of the Corps and the state relative to that project.

Each PPA must be completed and signed by the army and the state within a certain time frame to keep that project on schedule.

The Corps is dependent on the state to acquire land that is needed for construction of certain projects and, occasionally, for access to property to complete investigations. These responsibilities also must be achieved in a timely manner to keep projects on schedule.

The levee authorities, in many cases, own, claim or control the land needed for levees and flood walls, and are responsible for operations, maintenance and the integrity of levees and flood walls after construction completion.

The [U.S. Army] Corps [of Engineers] is building an unprecedented, state-of-the-art, 1.5-mile surge barrier with three navigable gates across the Gulf Intracoastal Waterway and the Mississippi River-Gulf Outlet.

Parishes and/or local governments in the HSDRRS are often responsible for granting rights of entry to property within their jurisdiction, and are occasionally called upon to create or amend local ordinances for variances in work schedules, such as night work, and allowances for temporary construction inconveniences such as increased noise levels.

If a parish or local government encounters problems getting a right of entry for construction, that project could be delayed.

Reaching the Goal

To reach the critical milestone and make the June 2011 goal, it is imperative that the Corps and all its partners provide their responsible actions in a timely manner.

There are other things that can affect the schedule and cause delays, such as worldwide demand for construction materials, bad weather including tropical events, changes in designs resulting in construction changes, landowner holdouts, concerns by special interest groups, and wildlife conservation concerns and studies.

The Largest Project in the World

The Corps is building an unprecedented, state-of-the-art, 1.5-mile surge barrier with three navigable gates across the Gulf Intracoastal Waterway and the Mississippi River-Gulf Outlet, the largest design-build civil works project in Corps history. It will be the largest project of its kind in the world.

Despite a four-month delay that involved design changes/improvements and navigational safety enhancements, that colossal project is on schedule to provide one percent risk reduction in June 2011. Working 24 hours a day and under lights at night, the contractor's crews have made up much of the lost time. "Our stepped-up production rate has been even more effective than we originally anticipated," said Col. Robert Sinkler, commander of the Hurricane Protection Office. "At this rate we expect to have much of the structure completed in 2010."

Additional Delays

Some projects in the HSDRRS that are planned for 100-year level accreditation in 2011 will have other continuing construction beyond that time. For example, the West Closure Complex—a project that will include the largest pump station in the world—aimed to be 100-year accredited in 2011 with work on other features continuing through 2013.

That huge project is now experiencing a two-month delay in its construction effort.

Though much effort occurred by an extensive team, the Corps did not receive the required real estate from the state and the levee authority by the June 1, 2009, milestone. Reasons for the delay were:

- On March 30, 2009, Congress and the administration designated Bayou aux Carpes an environmentally protected area as a part of the Jean Lafitte National [Historical] Park [and Preserve]. This happened just days before the Corps planned to acquire 9.6 acres of the property to build a flood wall as part of the West Closure Complex. The new designation required the Corps and state team to switch gears and produce the necessary documentation to complete a land swap with the Department of the Interior. Also,

- A private landowner at first agreed and then delayed granting right of entry for construction on his property, causing further delay.

"This project is now two months behind its goal to be 100-year accredited in 2011," said Col. Al Lee, commander of the New Orleans District, "but we are aggressively working with our construction teams to make up that time."

Temporary Structures Provide Interim Protection

The three outfall canals at 17th Street, Orleans Ave. and London Ave. are outfitted with interim pumps and closure structures that were installed before hurricane season 2006.

These interim structures provide 100-year level protection while the permanent canal closure structures are being designed. Construction completion on the permanent structures is planned for 2013. To provide the permanent replacements of these temporary facilities, the army and the state must sign a PPA by late August 2009. Any delay in signing the PPA could delay this project past its scheduled construction completion milestone of December 2013, putting the public at extended risk.

A Change of Plans

The Lake Pontchartrain levee continuation at the [Lake Pontchartrain] Causeway Bridge in Jefferson Parish presented an interesting situation for the Corps. The original Corps plan was to simply continue the levee through the Causeway intersection and build a roadway ramp across the levee. Further geotech analyses proved that an earthen ramp of this kind and in this location would require frequent maintenance and periodic levee lifts—ongoing and expensive procedures—because of expected settlement.

Another alternative the Corps considered was the installation of floodgates across the roadway that would be closed ahead of a tropical event. The Causeway Commission, the state of Louisiana, the levee authority and Jefferson Parish officials voiced opposition to that plan because of concerns with evacuation and the area's reliance on the Causeway as a major re-access to the city after an event.

A third alternative under consideration was the construction of a bridge over a flood wall, allowing traffic to remain continuous and uninterrupted. Even though this alternative meant more time for design and construction, as well as additional cost as compared to the gate, the Corps is recommending this engineering solution as the best alternative for risk reduction. The Causeway bridge over a flood wall is being designed now and is expected to be 100-year accredited by summer 2011, and completed by 2012.

Continued Improvements

Out of more than 350 contracts completed, planned or in construction for the HSDRRS, 13 contracts are currently projected to go beyond the June 1, 2011, goal. A year ago that figure was 27 contracts; but the team continues to improve and make progress. Over the past several months, 14 contracts were moved within the 2011 goal. As it stands now, 11 of those 13 contracts are projected to complete before the end of hurricane season 2011. The remaining contracts are projected to be completed before year's end 2011.

"More than 160 contracts have not yet been awarded," said Ms. Durham-Aguilera. "Until those contracts are awarded, the true construction duration is not known. The construction schedule we have now is a preliminary schedule, a working schedule. And we have been very conservative with our estimates, so we expect continued improvements."

Remember Hurricanes Gustav and Ike [in 2008]. The system held. And the system is stronger today than ever before.

Several contracts have been or will be awarded through the Early Contractor Involvement (ECI) process. This method enhances production and helps shorten the time frame of contract completion. "Using the ECI process," said Col. Sinkler, "we expect many of our contracts that now extend beyond June 1, 2011, to have a shortened duration because the design and pre-construction phases are occurring simultaneously."

Moving Ahead

Construction of a comprehensive *system* and the myriad of differing and evolving contracts results in a dynamic schedule that takes continued, dedicated effort to manage. "We look at the milestones every day," said Ms. Durham-Aguilera, "and every day we look for ways to improve and meet our June 2011 goal of providing a system that meets the 100-year level of accreditation.

"As with everything the Corps does, safety is our number one priority," added the director. "Should we have a tropical event while we are still in construction of the HSDRRS, we have interim protective measures for each unfinished project.

"Remember Hurricanes Gustav and Ike last year [2008]. The system held. And the system is stronger today than ever before."

New Orleans Is Not Safe from Hurricanes

Chris Francescani, Jim Avila, and Beth Tribolet

Chris Francescani and Beth Tribolet are senior producers at ABC News. Jim Avila is an ABC News senior law and justice correspondent.

New Orleans remains "alarmingly vulnerable" to large hurricanes, despite the $1.7 billion poured into the city to construct safeguards. The biggest problem is that the Mississippi River-Gulf Outlet (MRGO) built by the U.S. Army Corps of Engineers in the 1950s and '60s destroyed many miles of wetlands that had served as hurricane barriers. Although the Corps is attempting to rectify the situation, the city remains at risk. Some experts believe that some areas of the city must be abandoned since they cannot be made safe. Until the city is perceived as safe, it is likely that the population and businesses will not return.

After $1.7 billion worth of work on a patchwork of levees, pumps, flood walls, canals and floodgates, New Orleans as a whole remains alarmingly vulnerable to another Katrina-like catastrophe, according to scientists and engineers who have studied the improvements and residents, politicians and watchdogs who have spoken to ABC News.

Safer, Not Safe

"Is it safe?" asked Roy Dokka, professor of civil engineering at Louisiana State University. "It's safer, not safe. It's better than what we had before Katrina, but it isn't bulletproof."

[In 2007], two years after Hurricane Katrina, New Orleans' flood protection system remains a tangled paradox of hope and dread, strong and weak spots, reality and fantasy. Billions are flowing into the city's infrastructure coffers, and relentless scrutiny and testing has taught the U.S. Army Corps of Engineers some valuable lessons, but no one knows whether the massive and ongoing rebuilding efforts will outrun the next major storm.

Meanwhile, the city is slowly sinking while the sea is rising, and the state's wetlands barriers are disappearing faster than Louisiana could hope to rebuild them, experts say.

"Pre-Katrina, we weren't safe at all," said Oliver Houck, an environmental law professor at Tulane University Law School. "We just thought we were. Are we safer than that [now]? Clearly. But better than poor ain't great. And we are years away from being even good, much less great."

There seems to be a consensus that this is not where anyone wanted to see New Orleans two years after Hurricane Katrina.

The U.S. Army Corps of Engineers' Efforts May Be Flawed

Considerable criticism has fallen on the U.S. Army Corps of Engineers, which has been largely responsible for flood protection in New Orleans since the 1960s.

The corps contends that it has made dramatic improvements to the system and there's evidence it has in some places. The spot where the storm water surge broke through the Industrial Canal and flooded New Orleans' Lower Ninth Ward is one of the strongest, highest walls in the system now, though there is barely anyone left there to protect.

Other areas are said to be untested or weak. The corps is working with a $15 billion budget to come up with a flood protection plan that would shield the city from a 100-year storm by the fall of 2011. That's far less than half the strength of Katrina.

Supporters of the agency contend that it's doing the best it can under enormous political and logistical pressure. They say the corps's workforce splits its time and resources between short-term fixes to deal with immediate threats like the impending hurricane season and creating a long-term solution all the while crossing its fingers that the city isn't swamped with another major hurricane before it can complete its massive workload. Corps officials say they are hard at work at both assignments.

But critics in the local environmental science and coastal engineering communities say that the corps's entire mode of thinking largely in terms of structure building is outdated and fatally flawed.

"They're not the Army Corps of Nature," Tulane's Houck told ABC News. "They're the Army Corps of Engineers. They suck mud. They pour concrete. That's what they learn in school. That's what they go out and do. They're thinking levees. They're thinking pumps. They're thinking concrete. They're thinking 'beat nature. We're the nature-beating organization.' You go to their libraries, go to their [public relations] shops and just pull the films of the conquest of this or the conquest of that. They're conquistadores."

"You can't beat nature down here. You're going to have to live with it. You can't *beat* it. And the idea that we're going to build some kind of castle down here with big enough castle walls to hold out the Gulf of Mexico is fantasy," said Houck.

The Corps Failed to Protect New Orleans

While there was plenty of finger-pointing to go around at the time, Hurricane Katrina was largely viewed as a damning indictment of the corps's flood protection duties in the Crescent City [New Orleans]. Former U.S. Army Corps of Engineers commander and chief engineer Lt. Gen. Carl A. Strock publicly acknowledged as much in June 2006, when he said that it was a "catastrophic failure."

As a result, all the corps's work in New Orleans past, present and future has come under intense scrutiny from all sides, in and outside the government. The work has been studied, critiqued, debated and reviewed seemingly endlessly.

"We take input from a lot of people," said Karen Durham-Aguilera, the civilian director of Task Force Hope, the corps's hurricane protection system in New Orleans. "We deal almost on a daily basis with local governments, with levee authorities [and] with neighborhood groups, with the convention and visitors bureau, with the insurance industry."

"We answer to a lot of people," she said.

Post-Katrina Work

So after Katrina, the corps, in conjunction with a vast interagency task force, built a storm-modeling system that can track 152 different storm paths, ranging from a 25-year to a 5,000-year storm. It has used that modeling system as a blueprint to determine which areas in the city's flood protection plan are the neediest.

"We have strengthened levees," said Durham-Aguilera. "We have strengthened transition points were soil meets cement. We have improved flood walls. We have put surge barriers in. We have added pumping capacity. We have done a lot of things, and based on our various modeling, the hurricane system is better and stronger than it was prior to Katrina."

One key new feature of the system are floodgates along the northern wall of the city bordering Lake Pontchartrain, built in conjunction with new pumps so strong that corps officials say they can drain an Olympic-size swimming pool in seven to eight seconds. The agency is also planning a new drainage system that could substantially alleviate flooding in some parts of the city.

"This is a holistic approach," said the corps's Col. Jeff Bedey, commander of the corps's Hurricane Protection Office. "This is a systems approach to hurricane protection [and] not a system in name only, but truly a system."

One place where the system isn't working so well yet is St. Bernard Parish, the low-lying parish on the southeastern edge of the city.

The [U.S. Army Corps of Engineers] acknowledges the damage done [by the Mississippi River-Gulf Outlet], and the continued danger the parish faces from eastern-moving storm surges like Katrina.

The "Mister Go" Canal

Experts, studies and eyewitnesses say the most serious flaws in the rebuilt system of levees and flood walls are along the 76-mile Mississippi River-Gulf Outlet (known locally as "Mister Go") canal on the eastern edge of the Plaquemines/St. Bernard Parish region.

The MRGO [Mississippi River-Gulf Outlet] is a commercial/navigational canal built by the corps in the 1950s and 1960s as a shortcut between the Gulf of Mexico and New Orleans. It never brought in the commerce it was expected to, and inadvertently destroyed miles of barrier wetlands to its east in Lake Borgne. Those wetlands, environmental scientists say, were St. Bernard's natural protection against flooding.

"Why is it that we didn't drown for the past 500 years down here?" Houck asked. "We had this linear levee of wetlands between us and the Gulf. The storms just got knocked down before they got here."

The corps acknowledges the damage done, and the continued danger the parish faces from eastern-moving storm surges like Katrina.

"In the here and now today, we're not where we need to be and we acknowledge that," Bedey told ABC News when asked about the levee protection in St. Bernard Parish.

Wetlands Provide Protection

Environmental scientists say those wetlands were a crucial protection for St. Bernard Parish. The canal is now scheduled to be shut down and dredged. MRGO is widely blamed for driving Gulf storm surges right into the V-shaped funnel area on Lake Borgne and also overrunning St. Bernard Parish. The corps disputes this claim and says the closure of the canal is based on "economic and environmental reasons and not for any reason related to Hurricane Katrina," according to a news release issued earlier this month [August 2007].

This conflict is at the heart of the criticism of the corps's extensive efforts to rebuild a stronger flood protection system in New Orleans.

"No region in the country owes more to the corps for its very existence than this one," Houck said. "And no region has been more wrecked than this one by the Corps of Engineers and their mistakes. The problem is that the corps's new levee system program continues to create the same funnels and continues to rely on the same levees that destroyed the marshes around MRGO," Houck said.

"We lost 40,000 acres of marsh due to that one canal," he said. "That's a lot of levee protection. The cyprus swamps that were destroyed by the [MRGO] knocked down storm heights better than any canal you can imagine. But they're all dead. They're all gone. Now a project that restores levees around New Orleans is fine, but what you need to do is integrate in that project maximum cyprus rebuilding, marsh rebuilding, get those natural systems back below."

Bedey acknowledges the need to rebuild the wetlands, but says it's not as simple as critics are making it out to be.

"I can absolutely tell you that there is a core cadre of people, both internal and external to the corps, that are working day in and day out on that very issue. It's not as readily apparent as the 100-year level of protection where you see this [levee] right here, but the commitment is there. The work behind what we do? How we go about doing it? It's not as simple as a little puzzle."

The latest corps plan is to build some form of a barrier wall in Lake Borgne to prevent eastern-driven storm surges from pouring into the city. The plan may include a temporary floodgate at the mouth of the funnel.

Short-Term Options to Protect St. Bernard Parish

But shorter-term options are on the table too, and many New Orleans residents are demanding they be put in place. At an Aug. 9 [2007] meeting between the corps and two city council committees, several short-term solutions were discussed. One is to build a $100 million temporary gate near the mouth of the funnel. That project couldn't be completed until the start of the 2009 hurricane season, according to Bedey.

In the end, many of the most passionate experts say the only realistic way to "save" New Orleans is to scale it back and abandon some of the most low-lying areas.

Adding 3-foot plates to the tops of I-walls along the existing MRGO canal is another short-term option, at a predicted cost of $30 million to $50 million, but also can't be completed until 2009. But residents and politicians from battered St. Bernard Parish oppose the temporary gate, saying it'll push water back out into the lake and overrun MRGO, again flooding St. Bernard in a storm.

Bedey reportedly responded that the St. Bernard walls along MRGO would be fortified as part of the project. It was one of many objections that volleyed back and forth over virtually every option offered during the Aug. 9 meeting, according to news reports.

"Bedey said the agency hopes to decide within a few weeks whether to adopt any of the temporary fixes or to just hope that a major hurricane doesn't hit the city while the corps concentrates on completing a long-term plan to protect the city from the surge caused by a 100-year hurricane," the New Orleans *Times-Picayune* reported earlier this month.

Parts of New Orleans Are Too Dangerous

In the end, many of the most passionate experts say the only realistic way to "save" New Orleans is to scale it back and abandon some of the most low-lying areas.

"The problem is, 'Where's the leadership?'" asked Louisiana State's Dokka. "What are we going to do? To me there are certain places [in New Orleans] that are just too dangerous to live in, and they need to be partitioned like a ship. So then we can go [to] the rest of the country and say, 'OK, this is a dangerous place to live, but we're going to reduce the risk as much as we can.' There's stuff you can do, yes, but there's no leadership, because people are saying, 'We want to make it all better and put it back to what it was.' You can bring back New Orleans, but it'll be a smaller, but more resilient New Orleans."

An engineering expert from the Massachusetts Institute of Technology who has been deeply involved in reviewing the corps's work agrees.

"What I would like to see in some way is if there were more time to think about this, to think out of the box, to come up with solutions that don't rely on rebuilding bigger and better in the same footprint," said the engineer, who requested anonymity because he doesn't have approval to comment publicly on the progress of the flood protection system.

"You'd want to refocus strategy a little bit, and that may not be rebuilding in the same footprint."

"Rather than hope we can control nature, which I think in the end nature will always win, we need to live with nature in that respect and adapt to that," he said.

But how do you draw a community back home if you can't promise it protection? It's certainly a goal both the corps and its critics share.

"At the end of the day, this isn't about the 100-year level of protection," Bedey told ABC News. "This isn't about the wetlands. This is about helping to restore faith and confidence in the people, such that the people want to come back and the businesses want to come back."

5

New Orleans Cannot Be Made Safe from Hurricanes

Sheila Grissett and Mark Schleifstein

Sheila Grissett and Mark Schleifstein are writers for the Times-Picayune, *a daily newspaper in New Orleans.*

A report by the National Academy of Engineering and the National Research Council released in 2009 states that no matter how strong the walls and levees are around New Orleans, they will not be able to protect the city from extreme weather events. The experts agree that parts of the city must not be rebuilt since they cannot be protected. They also recommend that evacuation plans need to be improved, hospitals must be moved from dangerous areas, and all infrastructure needs to be upgraded.

A 100-year level of levee protection from hurricane storm surge is inadequate for a major city like New Orleans, and officials should consider relocating residents out of the most vulnerable areas, says a new report [April 2009] by the National Academy of Engineering and the National Research Council.

New Orleans residents need to recognize that no matter how high or sturdy they're built, the levees and flood walls surrounding the city cannot provide absolute protection against overtopping or failure in extreme events, the scientists and engineers concluded.

"A 100-year profile does not include a Katrina," said G. Wayne Clough, chairman of the peer review committee, referring to the standard used by the [U.S.] Army Corps of Engineers in its plans to improve the area's levee system by 2011.

"We believe the government should consider a higher level of protection, and not only for the levees in New Orleans, but also in Sacramento and other places where there are similar concerns," said Clough, who is secretary of the Smithsonian Institution and former president of the Georgia Institute of Technology.

New Orleans residents need to recognize that no matter how high or sturdy they're built, the levees and flood walls surrounding the city cannot provide absolute protection against overtopping or failure in extreme events.

Settlement in High-Risk Areas Should Be Discouraged

That also would mean changing the present National Flood Insurance Program standard of insuring properties from a 100-year event to require a higher standard for high-population areas like New Orleans, he said.

"As long as people can get insurance, they will rebuild," Clough said.

The report emphasized the need for reconsidering where people can live safely.

"The planning and design for upgrading the current hurricane protection system should discourage settlement in areas that are most vulnerable to flooding due to hurricane storm surge," the report said. "The voluntary relocation of people and neighborhoods out of particularly vulnerable areas—with adequate resources designed to improve their safety in less vulnerable areas—should be considered as a viable public policy option."

The report is the fifth and final peer review of the Army Corps of Engineers–sponsored forensic investigation of hurricane protection system failures in the New Orleans area during Hurricane Katrina.

That investigation by the 150-person Interagency Performance Evaluation Task Force [IPET] resulted in a 7,500-page, nine-volume study that detailed the reasons for levee and flood wall failures throughout the area, explained the risk of flooding if construction of the authorized levee system had been completed before Katrina hit and the chance of flooding with repairs in place as of June 2007.

Lessons from Katrina

The peer review generally praised the state-of-the-art IPET investigation and its results, and focused most of its comments on the lessons New Orleans and other communities can learn from the Katrina disaster.

Committee members used the report to urge that residents and local and national policy makers at least discuss not rebuilding in the region's most flood-prone areas.

"Reconstructing all pre-Katrina protective structures, and creating settlement patterns just as they existed before Katrina, simply would position the city and its inhabitants for additional, Katrina-like disasters in future big storms," the committee warned.

Ed Link, the University of Maryland engineering professor who heads the IPET task force, said that recommendation already has been adopted by the corps, as witnessed in its decision not to rebuild levees in lower Plaquemines Parish to the new 100-year requirements developed using the IPET report findings.

But Link said the decision to rebuild the levees surrounding east bank New Orleans and St. Bernard Parish on the footprint of the old levee system, with few changes, made sense because of the need to rebuild quickly and to reduce expenses.

Link said a number of the recommendations in the peer review report were incorporated in completing the summary and risk chapters of the IPET report after meeting with members of the peer review committee last fall.

Risks Can Only Be Minimized

Although the repairs and strengthening done since that August 2005 hurricane have reduced some vulnerabilities, the peer report stressed that the corps cannot build structures to eliminate all risks, only minimize them.

Locales below sea level are obviously at greatest risk of hurricane-driven storm surge flooding.

"The risks of inundation and flooding never can be fully eliminated by structures, no matter how large or sturdy," the committee said, noting that New Orleans presents a "special and complex" situation when it comes to hurricane preparedness and planning.

"There are large numbers of structures and residents in areas across the city near or below sea level. This situation poses considerable logistical challenges to relocation efforts, and it also prompts tough questions about the future of the city."

The report doesn't identify the areas that should be avoided, saying only that locales below sea level are obviously at greatest risk of hurricane-driven storm surge flooding. But the report did point to the ongoing corps Louisiana Coastal Protection and Restoration study, designed to recommend ways to protect New Orleans and the rest of the state's coastline from the equivalent of category 5 hurricanes, as the first step to answer some of those questions.

Alternatives in the draft version of that study outline large areas outside existing and proposed levee systems where a voluntary program of buyouts or raising of buildings above surge levels should be implemented.

The peer review committee warned of the need for a public discussion leading to development of new policies to tackle the politically touchy issue. But the report warned that in this fourth year after Katrina, it looks like the New Orleans region has returned to a policy of business and building as usual.

" . . . It appears that post-Katrina rebuilding activities are taking place largely according to the pre-Katrina hurricane protection system design without discussions of how a safer and more reliable design might be configured," the report said.

And where relocations aren't viable, the committee recommended major flood-proofing measures—starting with the elevation of buildings to at least the 100-year-flood level—and higher, wherever possible.

"If you're going to build in an area that has such a high risk of flooding, what can you do about it?" Clough said. "One can go back to what people did when they settled in New Orleans a long time ago—add an extra floor in building plans so that floor is expendable in a flood event."

The report also urged the IPET task force to hire a professional firm to write an easily readable layman's version of the IPET report that would better explain the concept of "residual risk" to local and state leaders and the public. Residual risk includes the potential for things to go wrong in the hurricane protection system, including failure of levees, walls, pump stations, or other features.

Link said the corps does plan to publish a new risk report aimed at explaining the protective features of the new 100-year improvements when they are completed in 2011.

The report also warned that the bureaucratic reality of changing administrations at the local corps office and local and state levee management agencies creates a risk that features of the IPET assessment, including studies of local geology, subsidence rates, and risk assessments, might be lost from their institutional memories. To combat that, it recommends the establishment of a public archive of IPET data and results.

Projects Must Be Externally Reviewed

The report also called for periodic, external reviews of the design, construction and maintenance of large, complex civil engineering projects such as the New Orleans levee system.

"A 'second opinion' allows an opportunity to ensure that calculations are reliable, methods employed are credible and appropriate, designs are adequate and safe, potential blind spots are minimized, and so on," the report said. "An outside external review group may also be able to state politically sensitive findings or facts that a government agency may be reluctant to."

Clough said those reviews also should take into account the potential for global warming to create more intense or more frequent hurricanes and higher sea levels.

In its examination of the IPET report's findings of the causes of the Katrina disaster, the peer review report found the IPET task force correctly concluded that, with the exception of four flood wall foundation design failures, all of the major breaches were caused by overtopping and subsequent erosion.

The reviewers agreed with the task force that designs for the 17th Street, London Avenue, and Industrial Canal flood walls were inadequate, and backed up a conclusion of the American Society of Civil Engineers' External Review Panel that "engineers routinely are expected to design for such conditions."

And the reviewers repeated a warning from an earlier report that there are still competing theories for the exact process in which the 17th Street canal wall failure occurred, and that the IPET's version, "while plausible, is not fully convincing."

In addition, the report recommends:

- strengthening critical public and private infrastructure, from water and electricity supplies to pumping stations and telecommunications;

- improving the region's evacuation plan with an eye toward more effectively protecting the ill and the elderly; and

- moving hospitals and nursing homes out of the most hazardous areas or armoring them to survive catastrophic events, and developing shelters to protect some residents without evacuations during hurricane events when major storm surges are not expected.

6

The Mississippi Coast Is Recovering from Katrina but Lacks Media Attention

Stan Tiner

Stan Tiner is the editor of the Sun Herald, *a daily newspaper in the Gulfport-Biloxi, Mississippi, metropolitan area.*

Although the Mississippi coast was severely damaged by Hurricane Katrina, most media attention has focused on New Orleans. It was the Mississippi coast, however, that received the full force of Katrina's winds and storm surge. Mississippi nonetheless has done a good job rebuilding after the storm, despite the news media's ongoing failure to completely report the story of Katrina and its aftermath. Residents of the Mississippi Gulf Coast want history to accurately report their role in both the disaster and the cleanup.

Three months after Hurricane Katrina, the *Sun Herald* described in a front-page editorial "Mississippi's Invisible Coast." It spoke of the fact that the further removed in time we were from Katrina, the less attention outside news reports paid to the plight of our region and its people, and the more it seemed history was being rewritten in a way that would render South Mississippi no more than a postscript to the greatest natural disaster to befall the nation.

Stan Tiner, "Will the History Books Be Accurate? Mississippi's STILL Invisible Coast," *Sun Herald*, September 6, 2009. Reproduced by permission.

Mississippi Is More than an "Add-on Phrase"

Already the trend had begun for the national media to cover South Mississippi's part of the story with an add-on phrase to the news of Katrina and its effects on New Orleans. We had been reduced to four words—"and the Gulf Coast."

That trend has become virtually universal now, and during the recent fourth anniversary media assessment of Katrina, the people of "the Gulf Coast" have receded into the hazy status of non-people whose story is untold.

This is troubling to the courageous people whose world was swept away on Aug. 29, 2005, and who have valiantly sought to recover and rebuild while struggling to survive.

Of course it is not possible to watch all of the national coverage of Katrina, but a substantial sampling clearly shows that New Orleans is THE story. It is troubling for those on our Coast to hear how New Orleans was "Ground Zero" for Katrina, or to see images of destruction in Pass Christian, Bay St. Louis or Biloxi shown while a broadcast focuses on New Orleans.

I will repeat the fact that Katrina's greatest winds and storm surge of more than 30 feet obliterated the Mississippi Coast and destroyed virtually all of the homes and businesses along its shore.

The terrible tragedy that befell New Orleans was the consequence of levee failures impacted by Katrina. Both New Orleans and Mississippi were the victims of the powerful storm, and both have tried to survive the years since with the individual efforts of our two states and the help of a generous nation.

Mississippi Is Recovering

Could the neglect of media to tell our story derive from the belief that everything is fine here, and there is nothing else to tell? It is possible, but were that the case you would think that would actually become the big story—how this poor little state was able to clean up, rebuild and get on with the business of life so quickly.

Wouldn't that become the model for all other disasters, the living textbook on how to get such a big job done in so short a period?

In fact, a good investigation of our situation would objectively show that a pretty good job has been done. It is a success built upon a long history of cleaning up and rebuilding after many hurricanes, good regional cooperation between local governments, and excellent leadership, from the governor's office to city halls across the Coast.

Also, it is in the DNA of local folks to tackle these problems with a strain of personal responsibility and energy that is among the best you will find anywhere.

Today's reporting ... will become tomorrow's history texts, and the evolving Katrina narrative is one of neglect toward our story and is increasingly likely to create a false or incomplete history of the great hurricane.

The Media Is Invited

OK, so the fourth anniversary has come and gone, and the Mississippi Coast is more invisible than ever in the media conversation about Katrina. Let us be hospitable and issue an invitation to reporters and newspapers and networks to come down next year for fifth anniversary coverage. Come stay a while and examine and report their findings as objective observers on the state of recovery in both places, New Orleans and the Mississippi Coast.

The fifth anniversary will offer a good benchmark to gauge how far each state has come, and, to the extent you discover a distinction in the progress between the two, it will be interesting to probe the reasons for the differences, and to report the combined lessons learned.

But beyond the studies of progress, it seems to many in our part of the world that there is an obligation on the part of the national media to get the story right in both breadth and depth.

There have been notable allies over the years, real advocates for our story—we salute Robin Roberts, Shepard Smith, Anderson Cooper and Kathleen Koch, reporters with roots in Mississippi—but over the sweep of time the media have told our story incompletely, if at all, and in doing so have really missed an important chapter in the history of the nation. After the storm, [the *Sun Herald*] begged for help, we shouted for attention, we did all we could to draw attention to our urgent plight and to gain support for our needs.

History Must Be Recorded Accurately

Today we are not asking for volunteers to come or for more financial or material assistance, but what we do fervently wish is that history be recorded fully and accurately. Today's reporting—print, broadcast and online—will become tomorrow's history texts, and the evolving Katrina narrative is one of neglect toward our story and is increasingly likely to create a false or incomplete history of the great hurricane and its aftermath.

This is a simple appeal to the better instincts of journalism that an effort be made to expose truth, and fairly report the fullness of human pain and triumph in Mississippi and of our stewardship of the national generosity that was given us.

That seems a modest request.

7

The Mississippi Coast Has Not Recovered from Katrina

Reilly Morse

Reilly Morse is a senior attorney for the Katrina Recovery Office of the Mississippi Center for Justice in Biloxi, and a founder of the Steps Coalition.

Hurricane Katrina is the greatest housing disaster in Mississippi's history, and rebuilding efforts in the coastal area have not been successful in providing adequate housing for low-income families. In addition, families who suffered significant wind damage to their homes have not yet been compensated, and have thus been unable to repair their homes. Although the state has provided housing vouchers to those in need, since there are not enough housing units to go around, the vouchers are sometimes useless. Moreover, several of the hardest hit communities are not allowing construction of public housing units to provide housing for low-income families. Although the state quickly funded repairs made by utility companies, it has been slow to help poorer citizens repair their properties.

At the fourth anniversary of Hurricane Katrina, the harmful consequences of Mississippi's misplaced priorities have become clear, and perhaps irreversible. The state has reduced its allocation for housing programs, lowered its forecasts for key affordable housing programs and abandoned plans for a full housing recovery. Between 2006 and 2008, the state reallo-

Reilly Morse, "Hurricane Katrina: Has Mississippi Fallen Further Behind? Trends and Challenges in Mississippi's Disaster Recovery," Steps Coalition, September 24, 2009. Reproduced by permission of the Mississippi Center for Justice and The Steps Coalition.

cated almost $800 million away from housing toward other purposes. Governor [Haley] Barbour claimed the diversion was justified because existing programs would fully address the housing crisis caused by Katrina.

Mississippi's Greatest Housing Disaster

In January 2009, however, the state received a report that anticipates over 15,000 fewer housing units from three key affordable housing programs than forecast by the state in May 2008. The report excuses this shortage on the assumption that fewer people will return to the Gulf Coast. This diverts attention from uncounted and still unserved people residing on the coast today and diminishes the coast's ability to welcome future residents. If we don't build enough permanent housing now, all of our people will not remain, whether it is working families, retirees, or any other residents. Neither the state's recent pursuit of 5,000 housing vouchers nor its program to permanently place cottages will bridge the gap. Unless Mississippi changes direction, it will have lost a unique opportunity to both recover from our state's greatest housing disaster and close disparities in housing conditions in the poorest state in the nation. This report traces the problems to their source and offers recommendations to restore affordable housing to its proper place as the state's first priority in disaster recovery.

Among other things, Mississippi

- lags Louisiana in its overall support for housing and rate of spending of disaster funds;

- started later and spent down less funds more slowly on affordable housing programs than for wealthier residents; and

- falls sharply below its own projections for production of affordable subsidized housing in small rental, long-term workforce housing, tax-credit financed rentals and public housing.

Failing to provide permanent, safe and affordable housing has profound human consequences. It means the absence of a fundamental human right that our nation expects other nations to observe with its internally displaced people. It means a deep uncertainty and insecurity in the most basic aspect of one's daily life. . . .

Failing to provide permanent, safe and affordable housing has profound human consequences.

Not Enough Affordable Houses

In August 2008, the Steps Coalition[1] warned that Mississippi's disaster housing recovery programs would not generate a sufficient supply of affordable housing to absorb the more than 4,000 households then in the FEMA [Federal Emergency Management Agency] temporary housing programs. One year later, this prediction tragically has come true, and there remain thousands of residents in this region who have unwillingly traded cramped FEMA trailers or hotel rooms for equally unacceptable housing "outside of the system," such as unrepaired or overcrowded dwellings shared with others. This unfortunate population joins thousands more wrongly denied or improperly removed from FEMA's temporary housing programs.

In the spring of 2009, Mississippi officials publicly acknowledged the need of the residents still outside the system and requested Congress to award 5,000 Section 8 housing vouchers. In support of this request, the state cited unmet needs for 2,000 pre-Katrina lower-income homeowners who are post-Katrina renters, 2,322 households who cannot afford rent due to the post-Katrina spike in rental rates, and 1,750 who await the completion of public housing. The Steps Coalition welcomes Mississippi's acknowledgement of unmet hous-

---

1. The Steps Coalition is a Mississippi-based social justice nonprofit organization working to rebuild Mississippi's Gulf Coast region.

ing need. But it was no invisible hand that pushed these households out of FEMA's temporary housing programs and into an abyss. Mississippi officials excluded thousands of wind-damaged homeowners and delayed programs to restore affordable rental and public housing.

HUD and Mississippi Are Failing

HUD [Department of Housing and Urban Development] and Mississippi share responsibility for flaws that have left thousands of households still without permanent housing four years after Katrina. With HUD's approval, Mississippi has denied compensation to thousands of lower-income wind-damaged homeowners, who now live in unrepaired housing or have been forced to become renters. Four years after Katrina, HUD and Mississippi have failed to deliver a large enough supply of affordable housing under the state's dramatically underperforming small rental and long-term workforce housing programs. Participants describe to the Steps Coalition deep frustration with complex, shifting, and excessively risk-averse requirements imposed by federal and state officials, their lawyers and accountants. Also, HUD has failed to heed Mississippi's appeal to apply common sense instead of bureaucratic rigidity to the important issue of duplication of benefits, which limits the ability of ordinary citizens to use the full spectrum of resources to achieve permanent housing.

HUD and Mississippi share responsibility to change current policies if the voucher program is to even partially fix self-created gaps in the housing recovery system. First, HUD awarded a grossly inadequate supply of vouchers to Gulf Coast housing authorities, less than 800 vouchers in response to a request for 5,000. Instead, HUD directed up to 2,500 to other housing authorities away from coastal Mississippi, which will worsen the lagging efforts to restore the population to pre-Katrina levels.

Second, a housing voucher without a rental unit is a ticket without a train. Mississippi asserted that there existed a nearly 25 percent vacancy rate and over 2,000 units of market-rate rentals whose landlords would accept Section 8 vouchers, a claim that was ridiculed when repeated by a HUD official in a congressional oversight hearing. Newly released data show a 12 percent vacancy rate in market-rent apartments. Raising further doubt on supply, Steps Coalition allies, Mississippi Center for Justice and Lawyers' Committee for Civil Rights Under Law, performed a field check of landlords accepting Section 8 vouchers and found fewer than 800 actual vacancies.

HUD and Mississippi must redouble their efforts to find innovative solutions to restore affordable housing. Extending compensation to households still struggling to repair their homes is a basic requirement. Mississippi added $10 million for housing resource centers to split among thousands of households that still face major gaps to recovery after exhausting all other resources. A substantially larger commitment is required.

HUD and Mississippi also must add to their commitments to income-targeted housing programs and, just as importantly, must simplify and accelerate the approval and implementation process.

Housing Vouchers Are Not Enough

As two congressional housing leaders reminded Governor Barbour, vouchers are "only one part of the housing equation; hard affordable housing units are also needed." Moreover, vouchers matched with market-rate rentals cannot take the place of long-term affordable housing units and do not represent a sustainable solution. Some housing advocates have called for the conversion of market-rate rentals to long-term subsidized rentals. The evidence of an overbuild is shown by the higher-than-normal market-rate vacancy rates and the first, modest softening in rental rates since Katrina. Mississippi could step in at this point to assist public housing authorities and other investors in subsidized housing in rebalancing and extending the affordability horizon of the area's rental market. To do so will require the state to return funds that were diverted away from housing to provide grants or loans to qualified buyers.

The Steps Coalition fully supports the call by Congressman [Barney] Frank and Congresswoman [Maxine] Waters for Governor Barbour to "match your commitment to vouchers with a commensurate commitment to the use of your existing CDBG [Community Development Block Grant] funds for the redevelopment and expansion of hard units of affordable housing in Mississippi."

Too Little Public Housing

The rate, speed and size of CDBG spending for the Gulf Coast's wealthiest homeowners dwarf spending for its poorest public housing residents. Until early 2008, public housing spending was so close to zero that it was nearly invisible. Mississippi took 18 months to spend more on public housing grants than it did on administration. The delay cannot be justified merely on differences in the size, grant amount, or complexity of the programs. Mississippi officials, and ultimately HUD itself, simply placed a lower priority on the state's most vulnerable residents than its wealthier residents.

State officials have routinely obscured the public housing picture by combining true public housing units with other forms of deep subsidy housing to artificially inflate the progress on traditional public housing. It is important to track conventional public housing separately because this category has the longest duration of affordability. The Gulf Coast area remains over 1,000 traditional public housing units below pre-Katrina levels, according to an independent rental market analysis. Only one unit out of 1,171 public housing apartments was vacant as of May, 2009, *a 0.1 percent vacancy rate....*

Mississippi still has a significant task ahead of itself in restoring traditional public housing capacity and meeting post-Katrina needs of this area's residents who earn at or below 30 percent of area median income. The obvious and basic immediate job ought to be to build at least 1,000 traditional public housing units affordable to the coast's most needy residents. The state's actual use of $105 million was not to restore public housing structures that have the longest affordability commitment, but to treat the fund as a bank to subsidize construction of shorter-horizon tax-credit properties. As tenants earning 30 percent of area median income are blended into properties with higher income eligibility requirements, the ability is lost to assure a one-for-one replacement of units permanently affordable to these tenants.

At least two municipalities in hardest-hit Hancock County have moratoria against construction of multifamily rental complexes, despite a clearly inadequate rate of housing recovery overall.

Not Enough Subsidized Rental Units

Mississippi has insisted from the outset that a surplus in apartment complexes financed by the Low-Income Housing Tax Credits (LIHTC) will expand public housing supply and offset shortfalls in its other affordable housing programs, such as the Small Rental Assistance Program and Long Term Workforce Housing. Unfortunately, this prediction also has failed to come true. According to one independent source, the Gulf Coast has produced 2,142 more LIHTC rental units than it had before Katrina, and expects another 1,242. But, the total from these programs would be only about 12,500 units, almost 11,000 fewer than the state originally predicted.

There remains strong demand for the subsidized rental housing available at LIHTC-financed apartments. In 2008, an independent rental market analyst pointed out that the unusually high occupancy rates and rapid lease-up rates at LIHTC-financed properties were indications of deep demand for affordable rental housing on the Mississippi Gulf Coast. Over the next year, the coast saw 1,450 LIHTC units added to the supply, and produced a temporarily inflated 11 percent vacancy rate while these units were being absorbed by the market. As occurred last year, this additional supply will be absorbed without exhausting remaining demand.

More aggressive enforcement of the federal Fair Housing Act would have accelerated the recovery of this important segment of the rental market. Through the Warm Welcome Gulf Coast campaign, a key Steps Coalition ally, Back Bay Mission undertook important educational work to dispel prejudice and educate the public about affordable housing. But education alone will not move some stubborn local governments. Federal and state officials have been all too timid in deferring to local moratoria against multifamily rental projects, or tax-credit finance projects. As a result, a permanent recovery has been delayed or denied to thousands of lower-income members of protected classes, including racial minorities, persons with disabilities, and families with children. As this report is released, at least two municipalities in hardest-hit Hancock County have moratoria against construction of multifamily rental complexes, despite a clearly inadequate rate of housing recovery overall. . . .

[In 2009], over 8,200 dwellings with major to severe damage remain unrepaired in the three coastal counties, according to the June 2009 update of the Mississippi Housing Recovery study.

Wind Damage Remains Unrepaired

The Steps Coalition looks forward to the release of the next phase of the Mississippi Housing Recovery Data Project's report on unrepaired damage. We anticipate confirmation that thousands of households still have unrepaired dwellings, both from storm surge and from hurricane wind damage. For a sizable percentage of wind-damaged homeowners who have not repaired their dwellings, the Steps Coalition anticipates the explanation will be inability to pay either due to inadequate insurance payment or absence of a federal grant program covering wind damage. . . .

Four years later, over 8,200 dwellings with major to severe damage remain unrepaired in the three coastal counties, according to the June 2009 update of the Mississippi Housing Recovery study. More than 4,500 of these unrepaired dwellings are not subject to elevation requirements, and so likely suffered primarily wind damage. In addition to the human toll of neglecting this population of storm victims, these unrepaired lots and structures will reduce property values and hamper neighborhood recovery.

Rural households above the three coastal counties continue to deteriorate in obscurity because the state has defined out of existence this entire category of disaster victims. The Steps Coalition renews its call for Governor Barbour to put forward some grant or compensation program to help wind-damaged Katrina victims to complete their recovery. From the standpoint of basic fairness it only makes sense for the state to extend similar concern to these citizens as it did to the utility companies whose repairs to wind damage to transmission and distribution lines in these same counties were promptly funded by hundreds of millions of dollars in federal CDBG assistance, without disdainful lectures about personal responsibility to insure one's assets against disaster.

8

New Orleans Must Be Rebuilt Sustainably

Mark Davis

Mark Davis is a senior research fellow at Tulane University Law School and the director of the Tulane Institute on Water Resources Law and Policy.

New Orleans is a city that became great because of its coastal location, despite the challenges such a location offers. Because climate change will force the same challenges on other locations in the United States, rebuilding a sustainable New Orleans that takes into account the stewardship of water and wetlands can serve as a model. Government projects that began in the 1960s are at the root of the devastation caused by Hurricane Katrina in that these projects destroyed wetlands and created development in below-sea-level locations. For New Orleans to survive, storm protection must be improved; wetlands must be restored; and communities must plan for their own well-being. Smarter land use and better building can allow New Orleans to be both resilient and sustainable.

New Orleans was built in a place that is both insane and inevitable. The culture of the city and the region is both parochial and cosmopolitan. The swamps and marshes that define the region's landscape seem timeless—even primordial—yet are mere thousands of years old and incredibly dynamic, geologically and hydrologically. New Orleans can be simultaneously inspiring, romantic, and frightening. No wonder virtual cottage industries of defenders and critics of the city and its future have emerged with such passion and numbers in the years since Hurricane Katrina roared across the landscape in August of 2005. In the bipolar world of post-Katrina New Orleans, I have found myself in both camps—sometimes on the same day—but I keep coming back to one fact: New Orleans was not an accident. It was not founded by mistake. It did not grow to be a great city by happenstance. It was not ruined by random forces.

Why New Orleans Is Important

That simple fact, the city's un-accidental nature, is what makes New Orleans important. It goes to the heart of why the struggles of New Orleans to survive and thrive matter. Just as New Orleans' past was not an accident, its future won't be accidental, either. Good or bad, it will be shaped by polices, decisions, and the appetite of its residents and this nation to accept hard truths and make meaningful commitments. These are the same issues the entire nation will increasingly face as we deal with rising seas, growing freshwater scarcity, and questions of who benefits and who suffers from climate change. If we can't figure out how to make New Orleans sustainable and resilient, it will be hard to imagine good things for other vulnerable places like Miami, Houston, and the New Jersey Shore. If we can't rebalance human development with the stewardship of water, wetlands, and other natural resources in New Orleans, it won't portend well for the Everglades, Chesapeake Bay, Great Lakes, and water-strapped cities like Las Vegas and Atlanta.

New Orleans did not just happen. America is filled with seemingly accidental cities—towns that grew around a mine, rail junction, factory, or as the result of some random upheaval. New Orleans is not that kind of town. Like London,

Venice, Amsterdam, Rotterdam, and Tokyo, it was founded in a challenging but essential place. Its proximity to the Gulf of Mexico and the Mississippi River combined with its modest but vital elevation (it was not below sea level then, though much of it is today) make New Orleans, as geographer Peirce Lewis has called it, an "impossible but inevitable city."

Its founders grasped the challenges and commercial advantages of building a city on a coastal swamp. New Orleans was not a daring experiment but rather one in a series of great cities founded and built in coastal plains and deltas. Or, as Jesuit historian Pierre François-Xavier de Charlevoix, an early chronicler of the French settlement, wrote in 1721: "On the banks of a navigable river, [near] the sea, from which a vessel can come up in twenty-four hours; on the fertility of its soil; . . . on its neighbourhood to Mexico, [to] Havana . . . can there be any thing more requisite to render a city flourishing?"

The vast alluvial plain that makes up most of the lower third of Louisiana went from relative equilibrium in 1900 to a net loss of over 1.2 million acres (and counting) of coastal wetlands since the 1930s.

The Balance Between New Orleans and Nature

The devastation from Katrina and Rita did not just happen. For much of its history, the match between New Orleans and nature was fairly, if grudgingly, balanced. The city grew and prospered, and the attendant risks were managed through its infrastructure, architecture, and grit. Without the benefit of federal flood protection or flood insurance, the city grew to greatness, its population reaching its zenith of nearly 650,000 in the early 1960s.

The balance began to shift in the early 20th century as efforts to drain wetlands (under the Orwellian banner of "reclamation"), manage river flows, and expand navigation took firm hold. Massive levees and drainage projects began to alter the landscape and seeded the vast coastal collapse that contributed to Katrina's devastating impact—complicating the plans for building a resilient city going forward. The vast alluvial plain that makes up most of the lower third of Louisiana went from relative equilibrium in 1900 to a net loss of over 1.2 million acres (and counting) of coastal wetlands since the 1930s. This was not wetlands merely being converted to dry land but land made vulnerable to open water.

Government Projects Make New Orleans More Vulnerable

These changes were driven in large part by government projects intended to spur economic development and provide flood protection. Many of the risks were known. In 1928, Percy Viosca Jr., a scientist working for the state of Louisiana, wrote, "Reclamation and flood control as practiced in Louisiana have been more or less a failure, destroying valuable natural resources without producing the permanent compensating benefits originally desired." Ironically, Viosca wrote this in the same year Congress enacted the Flood Control Act of 1928, which put the United States Army Corps of Engineers into the levee-building business for the first time and absolved them of liability for any consequences. As a result, the natural buffers that surround New Orleans began melting away.

For New Orleans itself, things changed dramatically when Hurricane Betsy hit in 1965. The flooding in some neighborhoods was much like that during Katrina, but the response could not have been more different. America had a larger appetite for public works back then. President Lyndon Johnson quickly enlisted Congress to pass a hurricane-protection system to guard the New Orleans area against the worst likely storm—a once-in-a-200-to-300-year event.

But the government settled for far less. The system that was actually built—and that ultimately failed—was the product of political and budgeting compromises, the failure to adapt to changing conditions and knowledge, and human error. The promises of storm levees and flood walls, combined with the risk-shifting aspects of the National Flood Insurance Program, led to changes in expectations and behavior. Low-lying areas were drained and developed, homes were built on slabs instead of being elevated, and less-water-resistant building materials were employed. The roles of natural defenses and individual and local responsibility were significantly downplayed, if not lost all together. After all, this was America, and we knew how to best nature. Perversely, the massive expenditure produced a city with more apparent protection, and less resilience. The net effect was a city at higher risk.

Decades of work and millions of taxpayer dollars actually exacerbated risk. And we must now face the fact that the tens of billions of dollars that have been committed to patching the failed system and rebuilding the devastated communities since Katrina could have the same effect—if important changes aren't made in the way protection, resilience, and community vitality are approached.

Sustainability Is Possible

A sustainable, resilient New Orleans won't just happen. New Orleans and much of the surrounding coastal region are incredibly vulnerable and currently unsustainable. Yet it is possible to significantly reduce that vulnerability and reestablish some worthwhile version of sustainability. This is true even in the face of rising seas, a collapsing coast, and the demonstrated failure of markets and government to get things right. But putting things right won't come from just building higher flood walls and levees. It won't come from just assigning blame for the failed levees and the disappearing wetlands. And it won't come from just the astounding energy and dedication of the people who and organizations that have come or returned to the Gulf Coast to forge a new future. We will revitalize the Louisiana Gulf Coast and encourage its displaced residents to return and stay—only if more confidence can be generated in the safety of the community. There are three essential elements of that security:

- Honest, effective, and purposeful storm protection.

- The conservation and restoration of coastal wetlands and barrier shorelines.

- Communities with the capacity to constructively engage in the planning and programs that affect their protection and well-being.

All of these things are interrelated, essential, and possible. And none of them exists in any adequate way today. Good projects, programs, and public accountability don't happen automatically or even because there is a consensus in favor of them. They are creatures—or victims—of laws and policies that shape public decision making. The planning, authorizing, budgeting, and funding process are all distinct and for the most part not currently tailored to the kinds of actions that the recovery and revitalization of New Orleans and the Gulf Coast will depend on.

Levees, pumps, gates, and wetlands are all essential elements to making New Orleans and its surrounding area a safe place to live. But how much and what kind of each of those things do we need, and what does "safe" really mean? Amazingly, those questions not only have not been answered, they really haven't been asked.

The degree of risk to New Orleans and to any vulnerable city is a function of two things: the consequences to human health and safety if the system were to fail and the probability of failure. The pace and extent of recovery for the region will depend in part on how well those risks are assessed and understood. No risk assessment was ever done on the New Orleans levee system prior to Katrina. It was impossible for people to actually know the level of risk with which they were living. Working, living, and investing here, as elsewhere, had become an act of custom and faith more than informed judgment. If New Orleans' levees had been built to the same standard of safety as federal law requires dams to be built, the odds of a failure resulting in the deaths of 1,000 people would be one such tragedy per 100,000 years. The levees of New Orleans were so under-designed and poorly maintained that their failure resulted in more than 1,000 deaths after only 40 years. Reclamation and flood control as practiced in Louisiana and now by the federal government remain a failure.

Progress Can Be Made

Yet, barring a direct hit by another Katrina in the next 30 to 50 years (an actuarially unlikely event) real progress can be made. But it has to begin now, and it has to begin with three things.

Over the next 20 or so years, any appreciable improvement protection and resilience will have to come from smarter building and land-use practices.

First, there needs to be an aggressive but realistic determination of just how safe and resilient New Orleans and other communities can and want to be as well as of the policies that are required. The current standard calls for New Orleans to be protected only against a one-in-100-year event, well below what Katrina was. This embarrassingly low threshold, met largely with existing pumps, levees, and flood walls, is pegged to the minimal requirements to qualify for coverage by the

National Flood Insurance Program. By comparison, the Netherlands plans for one-in-1,000-year to one-in-10,000-year risk horizons.

Second, it is time to get real about just how protected levees and pumps built by the Army Corps of Engineers and others can make us, and how soon. We can't simply build the Great Wall of New Orleans. There is not enough time, dirt, or money available, and the environmental and societal consequences from the impacts and displacement caused by the structures would, echoing Viosca's observation in 1928, be greater than the benefits. But we can have better protection and greater resilience for those times when water and trouble arrive—and they will—if our levees and flood walls are stronger and more reliable (not necessarily bigger) and the communities behind them are built smarter. Indeed, over the next 20 or so years, any appreciable improvement in protection and resilience will have to come from smarter building and land-use practices. A foot of water in a house on a slab is a disaster. A foot of water under a house raised 2 feet is an inconvenience. If that same house is in a neighborhood with natural sumps, modern cisterns and runoff controls, and well-protected utility infrastructure, it is just another bad-weather day.

Successful Rebuilding Must Create a Resilient Coast

Finally, it is essential to get serious about rising seas and the collapse of Louisiana's coast. There is no quick way to restore the million-plus acres of coastal lands that have already disappeared. Like engineered storm protection, this will take time and lots of money. It will also require a new and committed approach to managing wetlands, private property, and America's greatest river, the Mississippi. This must begin soon in earnest—if New Orleans is to have a fighting chance. Efforts to restore the coast have been under way for nearly 20 years. It has been noble work but more notable for what it has not achieved than what it has. This is not because we lack the knowledge and technology to do the job. Rather, it is because saving this place hasn't really been made anyone's job. It is someone's job to keep rivers deep and navigable. It is someone's job to tame and dominate water in the name of flood control and development. And it is someone's job to harvest the fish, game, oil, and gas that can be found in coastal Louisiana. Those jobs came first, and they don't go away just because we now want to do something new or do things differently. But until the whole range of those projects, programs, and activities are revisited and reconciled with the efforts to create a coast and communities that are sustainable and resilient, it is doubtful that any of the other efforts to rebuild, revitalize, and protect New Orleans will come to much.

New Orleans once again has become what it was to the French and British, to President Thomas Jefferson and President Abraham Lincoln—an essential city. The reasons, to be sure, are different, but it is essential nonetheless, because this is the proving ground for the American ideal of progress, equity, and reinvention. Can we honor our past without being prisoners of it? Can we muster the will and policies to apply the best of what we know to build safer, more resilient, efficient, and just communities? Can we forge a new bargain with nature rooted sufficiently in knowledge, respect, and humility to give phrases like "sustainable development" and "sustainable communities" real meaning? The future of New Orleans will depend on the answers to those questions, and the future of this country and many of its communities will depend on the answers to the questions raised in New Orleans. The right answers and actions won't come about by accident.

9

Mental Health Services Have Improved in New Orleans Since Katrina

Louisiana Department of Health and Hospitals

The Louisiana Department of Health and Hospitals is the state's primary public health agency.

New Orleans is undergoing a transformation of its mental health systems that promises to effectively deliver services where they are most needed through the opening of two new community-based clinics and a reorganization of inpatient services at area hospitals. Evidence-based models will guide the transformation. The changes promise to make services more accessible for families and allow more services to be offered in the home setting. Staff will be trained for their new responsibilities. The state remains committed to providing quality mental services for all residents.

As part of its ongoing plan to bolster and transform the public mental health system in the New Orleans area and the state, the Louisiana Department of Health and Hospitals will soon [2009] open two, new community-based clinics in the city; add new, high-end child/adolescent outpatient services to its network; and move inpatient services from a state hospital in Uptown to one in St. Tammany Parish.

Changes to the city's community-based infrastructure began last year under the direction of Gov. Bobby Jindal and

Louisiana Department of Health and Hospitals, "DHH Details Next Step in Improving Mental Health Services in New Orleans," Louisiana Department of Health and Hospitals, July 17, 2009. www.dhh.louisiana.gov. © 2009 Louisiana Department of Health and Hospitals. Reproduced by permission.

DHH [Department of Health and Hospitals] Secretary Alan Levine, and included the infusion of millions of dollars of new state money, the implementation of new evidence-based community treatment services and child/adolescent crisis response teams, the reform of the Metropolitan Human Services District and the passage of legislation to strengthen the public safety component of the mental health system.

With the additional reforms being implemented this year, New Orleans will undergo the most significant transformation of its mental health system in recent history. The city and the state will move closer to the evidence-supported models employed by other states, which have reduced their reliance on inpatient services while increasing family contact in the community and home setting.

The new outpatient services will be located closer to the people who use them—in two clinics on public transportation routes in neighborhoods on both sides of the river, and even, in some cases, in residents' homes. These access points were shut down after Hurricane Katrina, and will now be made available again.

More Effective Care

DHH announced in March of this year that it would deliver more effective hospital care at a more efficient cost to the state by merging its inpatient mental health operations at the New Orleans Adolescent Hospital [NOAH] into Southeast Louisiana Hospital.

Combining the mental health operations of NOAH and Southeast allows DHH staff to separate units for adolescents and children—a national best practice that the agency had not been able to institute before at NOAH or Southeast because patient counts at both were too low.

Both the child and adolescent patient groups will benefit from hospital treatments redesigned for their appropriate developmental stages and ages, rather than something aimed for the middle ground.

To guide the tasks and activities needed to make the merger happen and ensure that all patient and staff concerns were considered and addressed, the state formed a steering committee consisting of representatives from NOAH and Southeast.

Representatives included the chief executive officers, medical directors and directors of nursing services of each hospital; the clinical director, hospital services director, and acute unit and youth services coordinators from Southeast; the social services director of NOAH; and the fiscal and human resources directors from the state's regional department.

The steering committee, in turn, created task groups in four key areas: client care, staffing and support services, physical plant (hospital buildings and facilities), and contracts. The client care task group has worked to develop an integration plan which optimizes the services available to clients.

As patients are discharged from NOAH, the vacant beds are closed and a corresponding number of beds at Southeast are opened.

Three vacant adult beds have already been moved. On July 20, five child/youth beds and five adult beds will move from NOAH to Southeast, to be followed by five more adult beds on July 27. Five child/youth beds and seven adult beds are scheduled to move August 3.

While it is expected only a few child and adolescent patients may be moved from NOAH to Southeast, the client care task group identified case managers from both hospitals to work with families and/or custody agencies of these patients to ensure awareness and understanding of how care will be continued.

Children who receive treatment in state hospitals also receive educational support from the state. The steering committee has been working closely with the area Special School District coordinator to assure that the education these patients' receive is uninterrupted.

DHH is also offering transportation to and from two new outpatient clinics on the East and West Bank to Southeast. Transportation from the new outpatient clinics, one in Mid-City and one in Algiers, to Southeast is scheduled five days each week, including Saturday and Sunday. The schedule will be evaluated periodically and revised as needed.

New Staff Responsibilities

The changes taking place in the mental health care system in the Greater New Orleans area require a shift in staffing, including job transfers from NOAH to Southeast and to the two new outpatient clinics in Mid-City and Algiers, and a layoff of some state employees at NOAH.

Of NOAH's total workforce, about 141 employees will transfer to Southeast or one of the new outpatient clinics to open in Orleans Parish. Some employees—no more than 49—will be laid off. The total layoffs will most likely decrease from 49 due to early retirement or resignations.

Inpatient workers needed to staff beds will transfer to Southeast as beds are moved to Southeast, while outpatient staff will transfer when the new clinics open.

To help employees who will be transferring from NOAH to Southeast, the nursing and education departments of both hospitals have been collaborating on orientation and training schedules to accommodate the gradual transition of staff while assuring workers are prepared to assume their new responsibilities in their assigned unit. All orientation takes place through the respective departments of their assigned unit, i.e., nursing services, social services, etc.

To help employees who will be laid off, DHH will offer outplacement services, including counseling and employee assistance services. All layoff processes will be conducted in accordance with Civil Service Rules and guidelines, which govern state employment, under the oversight of the Department of Civil Service and the Department of Health and Hospitals Human Resources.

According to Civil Service Rules, all impacted employees must be given a general layoff notice and five calendar days to review them before Civil Service can approve the plan. The general layoff notice was delivered July 15.

If Civil Service approves the plan as submitted, a final layoff notice will be delivered to each impacted employee in late July, and layoffs will be effective August 14, 2009.

Clinics and Services Are More Available for Families

With an investment of more than $14 million in new services in 2008, the state introduced to New Orleans highly proven services such as Assertive Community Treatment (ACT) and Forensic Assertive Community Treatment (FACT) teams, a Child and Adolescent Response Team (CART), a Supportive Housing Program and a Mental Health Emergency Room Extension/crisis receiving service.

These services, new to New Orleans, have made it possible for hundreds of area residents to receive evidence-based mental health treatment in their homes and communities rather than in institutions, and have provided additional supports, such as housing assistance, that help people with mental illness achieve stability in ways that treatment alone cannot provide.

These therapies not only produce better results in a more dignified manner for patients and their families, but can be delivered much more cost-effectively than hospital-based services.

Additional new outpatient services coming soon feature some of the most highly regarded, evidence-based outpatient treatments currently in use nationwide.

These include mental health therapies such as Dialectical Behavior Therapy (DBT), which has been proven through years of research to result in 50 to 60 percent reductions in suicidal thoughts and behaviors among child and adolescent patients and 40 to 70 percent reductions in the rate of rehospitalization for patients who have been hospitalized previously. These are remarkable outcomes that can be delivered through community-based programs in outpatient clinics.

New Services to Be Offered in Homes

Other new or expanded services will include Multisystemic Therapy (MST) and Functional Family Therapy (FFT), which will be offered in homes.

These therapies not only produce better results in a more dignified manner for patients and their families, but can be delivered much more cost-effectively than hospital-based services.

The state is now completing renovations of the new Mid-City outpatient clinic, which will be known as the Mid-Town Child/Adolescent Behavioral Health Center, and expects to open by mid-August. The center will serve as the outpatient clinic for the East Bank of Orleans Parish, and will feature:

- screening and assessment services,

- psychiatry and medication management services,

- parental counseling,

- life skills treatment for youth, and

- substance abuse prevention and treatment services.

The Office of Mental Health has contracted with the Tulane University Department of Psychiatry to provide both psychiatric and psychological services at the center.

A second new outpatient clinic in Algiers will open by the end of August. The Algiers Child/Adolescent Behavioral Health Center will house the regional administrative offices for DHH's Office of Mental Health and will serve as the outpatient clinic for the West Bank of Orleans Parish and for St. Bernard and Plaquemines parishes, featuring:

- screening and assessment services,

- psychiatry and medication management services,

- parental counseling,

- life skills treatment for youth,

- substance abuse prevention and treatment services, and

- a mobile van for community-based services.

The Office of Mental Health has contracted with the LSU [Louisiana State University] Department of Psychiatry to provide both psychiatric and psychological services at the center.

The Louisiana Department of Health and Hospitals serves to protect and promote health statewide and to ensure access to medical, preventive and rehabilitative services for all state citizens.

Both the Mid-Town Behavioral Health Center and the Algiers Behavioral Health Center will share a new "Access Unit," a service that manages community-based treatment for children and youth who may be dangerous to self and/or others. The Access Unit will be available at each facility.

Until these new clinics open, outpatient services will continue to be provided at NOAH and Chartres-Pontchartrain outpatient services clinic.

The transformation of mental health services is an ongoing priority of DHH, guided primarily by data and evidence shown to be effective in other states.

The Louisiana Department of Health and Hospitals serves to protect and promote health statewide and to ensure access to medical, preventive and rehabilitative services for all state citizens.

10

Post-Katrina Mental Health Services Are Still in Crisis

Stephanie Smith

Stephanie Smith is a CNN medical news producer.

Since Hurricane Katrina struck New Orleans in 2005, mental health problems among residents have continued to increase while resources to treat these problems have diminished. Less than half the number of in-patient beds available before Katrina are available in 2009. Although community-based clinics will fill an important need for outpatient care, they cannot replace inpatient hospital beds needed for when a patient has a psychotic breakdown or is suicidal. The closure of the New Orleans Adolescent Hospital is of particular concern since it is the only remaining mental health facility in New Orleans.

As the storm raged outside her hospital room four years ago, an equally consuming force hijacked Alesia Crockett's mind: deep depression.

For days, Crockett lay in darkness and a tangle of sweaty hospital bed sheets, one among hundreds of desperate patients trapped inside Charity Hospital in 2005, while outside, Hurricane Katrina and its aftermath battered the city.

Crockett had been admitted to Charity's inpatient mental health unit after having a psychotic episode. She had struggled for years with bipolar disorder, an illness that causes her to volley between euphoria and profound depression.

Stephanie Smith, "4 Years After Katrina, NOLA Mental Health System Still in Crisis," CNN Health, August 28, 2009. www.cnn.com. © 2009 Cable News Network. Reproduced by permission.

She said she barely remembers Katrina.

"Most of the time, I was in a fog, but I do remember some things," Crockett said. "Where my room was, I could see thousands of people wandering, and I could see the waters rise."

While mental health problems grow, the resources to treat those problems continue to wane.

Mental Health Problems Increase

Crockett, and many other New Orleanians suffering from chronic mental illness—and those with what is called "soft depression," or non-chronic mental illness—say Katrina may have relented days after it hit New Orleans proper, but their mental health issues have not.

"Four years later, everything is not all right in New Orleans," said Dr. Jan Johnson, a psychiatrist who treats Crockett.

While mental health problems grow, the resources to treat those problems continue to wane.

A report about mental health issues in New Orleans after Katrina, published in early 2008 in the journal *Psychiatric Annals*, lists the number of inpatient psychiatric beds in greater New Orleans at 487 before the storm. Since Katrina, that number has declined to 190.

Most of the remaining beds are dedicated to patients unable to live independently. That leaves what the report's authors describe as a "paltry" 17 beds for acute mental health care in New Orleans.

"The situation is unconscionable, atrocious. I can't use enough bad words to describe it," said Johnson, who is an associate professor of clinical psychiatry at the Tulane University School of Medicine. "Patients are not getting care, they are sitting in emergency rooms for days, and that's just an inappropriate place for psychiatric patients."

For two years following Katrina, after being rescued from Charity, Crockett's illness was controlled with medications. Then in 2007, she stopped taking them, and she had another episode.

"She came to my clinic and was psychotic and really a danger to herself not able to care for herself," Johnson said. "And I had nowhere to hospitalize her."

After leaving the clinic, Crockett bounced among three local hospitals before being transported to the closest medical center with an available psychiatric bed, several hours outside of New Orleans.

> *The system has been in horrible shape for a while. . . . We had our problems even before the storm, but comparatively, we had it much better then. It's very frustrating.*

"I can remember being in the back of an ambulance, and I kept thinking, 'This is taking so long,'" Crockett said. "I didn't know where I was going. I just remember seeing the sky turn from daytime to nighttime, and we still hadn't gotten there."

Crockett is far from alone, Johnson says.

"The system has been in horrible shape for a while," she said. "We had our problems even before the storm, but comparatively, we had it much better then. It's very frustrating."

The Deadly Consequences

And the consequences of not finding a bed for acutely ill patents can be deadly.

In January 2008, a New Orleans police officer was killed by a man suffering from psychosis due to schizophrenia, New Orleans police said. The officer, Nicola Cotton, approached 44-year-old Bernell Johnson for questioning about a rape. A struggle ensued, and Johnson overpowered and killed Cotton with her own gun, police said.

As it turns out, Johnson was no longer under psychiatric care and was not taking his prescribed medication.

Cotton's death trained a spotlight on the deplorable condition of the New Orleans mental health system—for a moment—said Rep. Neil Abramson of the Louisiana House of Representatives. Months after Cotton's death, Louisiana allotted millions of dollars to bolster mental health services in New Orleans, he said.

A year later, the funding was gone.

"People are outraged," Abramson said. "Everyone is concerned about consequences you can't quantify. Safety of law enforcement personnel, more psychotic patients out on the street, and more killings instead of people getting the treatment they need."

Fighting the Closure of New Orleans Adolescent Hospital

Abramson is fighting to get back critical inpatient beds. At the center of that fight is the New Orleans Adolescent Hospital (NOAH), which is scheduled to close Tuesday [September 1, 2009]. After Cotton's death in 2008, legislators allotted $14.2 million to NOAH, Abramson says. This year, Gov. Bobby Jindal line-item vetoed that funding.

"That's why this is so critical," Abramson said. "This is the only state-operated mental health facility left in New Orleans. And now there will be none."

Louisiana Department of Health and Hospitals spokesperson says that the veto was justified, and that funding appropriated to NOAH would have resulted in a loss of beds at another local hospital.

"This is much bigger than closing NOAH," said Alan Levine, secretary of the Louisiana Department of Health and Hospitals. "We have to put mental health resources where we know they have the highest opportunity to succeed."

Levine called the debate about NOAH and inpatient beds among New Orleans caregivers and legislators symbolic of overall frustration with mental health care in the area, adding that Louisiana is focusing funding on community-based services, rather than inpatient beds, a strategy that he says will eventually shore up New Orleans' mental health system.

Jan Johnson, the New Orleans psychiatrist, agrees about the need for more community-based services.

"It's part of the answer, but it in no way can really take the place of hospital beds that we need," she said. "Someone with diabetes may be managed outpatient, but if they have a heart attack as a result of it, they need an inpatient bed. Our patients are the same way. We can manage a lot of this outpatient and community-based, but when they have an acute psychiatric episode or they are suicidal, they need an inpatient bed."

Today, Crockett, Johnson's patient, is well. But sometimes, fears about tomorrow creep up on her.

"I wonder sometimes, if I were to get sick, where would I go?" Crockett said. "We are people battling an illness, and we don't need to also have to be faced with not having the availability of beds and hospitals and doctors. If I want the help that I so desperately need, I can't get it because it's not there."

11

Post-Katrina School Reform Has Been Successful in New Orleans

Rick Jervis

Rick Jervis is a reporter for USA Today.

At new schools such as Langston Hughes Academy, New Orleans students are improving test scores and performance. Although the New Orleans schools were some of the worst in the state of Louisiana before Hurricane Katrina, post-Katrina reforms, including charter schools, have met with success. More than half of the students in New Orleans now attend charter schools. Charter schools do not need to have school board approval for the hiring and firing of teachers, and they are free to set their own curriculum. In addition, charter schools operate without teachers' unions.

The devastation of Hurricane Katrina four years ago brought with it many changes for this city, but perhaps its most enduring mark may be the new charter school system that came cascading in during the storm's aftermath.

Take, for instance, the students at Langston Hughes Academy. Once struggling to meet state testing standards, they're getting a lot of help to try and do better. Their learning environment has changed to one with electronic blackboards and teachers hailing from Ivy League schools.

The talk here is not about where to go after school, but where to go to college.

Rick Jervis, "High Marks for New Orleans' Charter Schools," *USA Today*, August 26, 2009. Copyright © 2009, USA Today. Reproduced by permission.

"There are higher expectations now and no excuses," said John Alford, the Harvard-trained leader of the school. "Kids are starting to see college more as a reality, a real option."

New Orleans' school district's performance score—a tally of test scores and other performance measures—jumped from a 56.9 pre-Katrina to 66.4 [in 2008].

Charter Schools in New Orleans

Langston Hughes Academy is one of 52 charter schools operating in New Orleans, which also has 37 traditionally run schools. Nearly 60% of the city's public school students attend charter schools—the highest percentage of any American city. School district officials hope to raise that percentage to 75% in the coming years.

New Orleans' school district's performance score—a tally of test scores and other performance measures—jumped from 56.9 pre-Katrina to 66.4 last year [2008] according to state Department of Education figures. Statewide, the average during that same period stayed roughly the same: 87.4 pre-Katrina and 87.2 last year.

The numbers suggest the city still has some catching up to do with the rest of the state. Determining how New Orleans stacks up with the rest of the nation is difficult to assess since the tests are particular to Louisiana and comparisons cannot be reliably made with similar tests in other states.

Even so, the revamping of New Orleans schools, some of the worst-performing in the nation pre-Katrina, is catching the attention of educators nationwide, said Tony Miller, deputy secretary of the U.S. Department of Education. "If these types of practices can be taken across the country, especially in some of the more challenging urban environments, that would make a difference in improving education," Miller said during a recent visit to New Orleans. "You're seeing some of those results here."

The Charter School Difference

Charter schools are public schools that use a mix of taxpayer funds and privately raised dollars to run their schools, said Paul Vallas, superintendent of the Recovery School District, which took over the city's worst-performing and flood-wrecked schools. They're free and open to all students but are independently managed by individuals or corporations. They run much the way businesses are: competing for students, top teachers and fund-raising dollars.

They differ from traditionally run schools in that they have the autonomy to hire and fire staff and set their own curriculum without school board approval. Charters also have longer school years—almost 11 months—and longer days than traditional schools.

Charter schools' business models, and competition between themselves, don't allow for the sharing of successful techniques throughout the district, said Larry Carter, president of the United Teachers of New Orleans, the local union.

"There's no replication of programs that are successful," Carter said. "I don't want to see schools closing year after year because their business models don't work."

Luis Mirón, director of the Institute for Quality and Equity in Education at Loyola University [New Orleans], said the success of what he called the "charter surge" has been based on temporary measures—a recovery school district that will eventually return schools to the Orleans Parish School Board and millions in federal recovery dollars, he said.

"It's been extraordinary as far as student achievement," said Mirón, who is also dean of Loyola's College of Social Sciences. "The question is: After the recovery money runs out, how do you sustain that reform?"

Many charter school leaders say they're in for the long haul. Ben Kleban, another Harvard-trained educator, traded a rising career as a financial planner for Boeing to get into the charter school business. Today, he runs the New Orleans College Prep charter school in the Central City neighborhood.

Each morning, nine buses shuttle 460 students to the school from all corners of the parish. That's a rise in attendance from 100 students two years ago.

On a recent afternoon, Kleban inspected a quiet line of uniformed kindergarteners exiting the cafeteria after lunch, pointing out how every shirt was tucked in and every shoe the same color.

"They're professionals," Kleban, 29, said of the students. "You don't see that in every public school you walk into."

Charters began sprouting in New Orleans when the traditional school system was in tatters, said Jeanne Allen, president of the pro-charter Center for Education Reform in Washington.

Charter schools take away politics, she said. Hiring teachers, for instance, can be done without unions or school boards, Allen said.

12

Post-Katrina School Reform Has Not Been Successful in New Orleans

Craig Chamberlain

Craig Chamberlain is the editor of education for the News Bureau at the University of Illinois.

Luis Mirón, currently the director of the Institute for Quality and Equity in Education at Loyola University in New Orleans, has conducted a study that points to serious inequities among the schools opened in New Orleans after Hurricane Katrina. Schools serving middle-class students were opened quickly while those serving low-income students were not opened until later. In addition, the community was not involved in the establishment of charter schools, nor was there careful planning of curriculum. It is likely that many teachers hired by the Recovery School District will be under-qualified as well. Mirón's report concludes that school reform should come from within, not be imposed by the state, to be successful.

Can a devastating flood set the stage for the transformation of a school system?

Many saw an opportunity to find out in New Orleans in the wake of hurricane Katrina last August [2005]. The state took over most of the city's schools and began an effort to reopen as many as possible as charter schools.

The result is "one of the most massive experiments in urban education ever conducted," according to Luis Mirón, an

Craig Chamberlain, "Professor Sees Inequity, Little Change, in Post-Katrina School Reform," News Bureau, University of Illinois, August 23, 2006. Reproduced by permission.

education professor at the University of Illinois at Urbana-Champaign, and a New Orleans native, who has advised and studied New Orleans schools for 20 years.

Troubling Inequities

Mirón has documented and studied the progress of that "experiment" during the year since Katrina, with help from graduate students Robert Ward and Maria Lovett, and so far is not encouraged by the results. He has seen troubling inequities in the way schools have been reopened, evidence of serious underfunding of the charter schools that have been opened, and few real improvements in the curriculum or in classroom instruction.

With a new school year beginning, the state-run Recovery School District, serving most of the city's low-income and at-risk students, finds itself scrambling to find the teachers it needs—many likely to be under-qualified—for thousands of expected students.

[Education professor Luis Mirón] has seen troubling inequities in the way schools have been reopened, evidence of serious underfunding of the charter schools that have been opened, and few real improvements in the curriculum or in classroom instruction.

Central to some of these problems is that the state never took the time or did the outreach to get "buy-in" from the community or teachers for the charter school concept, Mirón said. That buy-in is "ultimately what makes any of these reform models go," he said. "Charter schools won't work without that level of community involvement."

Not Enough Time Spent on Curriculum

They also never took the time or did the hard work to plan a new curriculum that would raise the level of instruction, Mirón said.

"One of the lessons from this is don't wait for a hurricane" to start implementing school reforms, Mirón said. "Take the time to do it and fund it adequately . . . invest early on into innovation and reform, rather than wait for a crisis or catastrophe."

The argument could be made, Mirón said, that the state had to move fast just to get schools reopened, and didn't have the luxury of time for involving the community or planning real change.

"But that argument doesn't hold much weight, because the state was very slow to open up schools," even when resources were clearly available to do so, he said. On the other hand. "the state was very fast to license and approve charters."

A group of schools on the West Bank section of New Orleans, serving mostly middle-class students and a large proportion of "gifted and talented" students, was quickly turned into charter schools and, with federal help, reopened by January, Mirón said. During the same time, several thousand low-income and special needs students were unable to attend school at all because of lack of access or transportation, he said.

"The reason they moved so fast is because they wanted to get the charter school model—this flexible, privately governed model—away from the public school board, a majority-black, elected school board, and put it in the hands of independent private organizations," he said.

New Orleans Schools Needed Reforming

Mirón said he agreed with the general consensus before Katrina that the New Orleans schools were failing and in need of serious reform. For at least two decades, "the school system had resisted every single reform that came out the door," he said, and the city, with its fragmented politics, "could never get behind a single vision for its schools."

Mirón began following developments in New Orleans schools as a staffer with the Bureau of Governmental Research in New Orleans during the mid- to late-1980s, when he developed educational policy proposals for the school system. He then became a professor in the Urban Education lab at the University of New Orleans, where he also worked on reform efforts with schools in the system. He has continued to study developments in the system as he moved to new academic posts in California and Illinois.

"I'm still optimistic that New Orleans will be better off post-Katrina with the charter model than they were pre-Katrina, but time is a valuable resource," Mirón said. The city and the state may have lost anywhere from one to five years in its attempts so far to transform the schools, he said, "but I do believe that it's still salvageable."

State Takeover Should Be Avoided

One lesson from New Orleans, Mirón said, is to avoid a state takeover in any similar effort at reform. "They clearly had alternatives," he said. "The state takeover model is really the model of last resort. . . . Change should come from within, in participation with the community."

When the state took over, it thought it would get hundreds of applications to run charters, but it didn't, Mirón said. The review process then took much longer than expected, and only a handful of charter schools were established. The state-run Recovery School District is now "in an absolute mess," and rushing to open 50-plus schools for the fall, he said.

"The whole irony of this is that what the elite business community in New Orleans wanted—which was to get control of the schools out of the hands of a central bureaucracy—is exactly what they seem to have unintentionally created in the Recovery School District," Mirón said.

Likewise, the state sought to establish charter schools in order to avoid running the schools itself, "but guess what—that's exactly what they're doing now," Mirón said.

13

Post-Katrina School Reform in New Orleans Shows Mixed Results

Sarah Carr

Sarah Carr is a journalist who reports on educational issues for the Times-Picayune, *a daily newspaper in New Orleans.*

While some charter schools such as the Langston Hughes Academy show progress in education reform in New Orleans, other schools such as Israel M. Augustine Middle School remain damaged and unopened, serving as homes for squatters. Some forty schools in the Recovery School District remain unused, although equipment, furniture, and student records such as test scores and birth certificates remain in the schools that continue to deteriorate while school officials haggle with the Federal Emergency Management Agency over funding. Thus, while Langston Hughes Academy represents the recovery of education in New Orleans, Israel M. Augustine Middle School illustrates how much more must be accomplished.

Earlier this week [August 2009], a who's who of state and city officials, from Gov. Bobby Jindal to Mayor Ray Nagin, gathered to dedicate the first new public school building to open in New Orleans since Katrina.

Inside Langston Hughes Academy, a light-filled atrium led the way to the hallways and classrooms of a state-of-the-art

95

building whose magnificence was unimaginable among New Orleans' crop of public schools five years ago, many of them already decaying. Completed in less than two years, the fast-tracked project crystallized the city's progress since Katrina.

A few miles away, in the heart of the city and across the street from the well-trafficked criminal court complex, a stair-case covered with stinking takeout food containers, swarms of flies, underwear and broken strings of Mardi Gras beads leads the way into the Israel M. Augustine Middle School building.

If Langston Hughes represents progress, Israel Augustine—largely untouched over the past four years, except by squatters—represents its opposite.

From the classroom with music notes still illustrating the single-stroke drumroll to the clocks whose hands stopped at 5:10 when the power went out, the building evokes a city and people who remain, in some ways, frozen in time.

Some of the most haunting reminders [of Katrina] can be found in New Orleans' empty school buildings, a number of which remain in limbo as school officials negotiate with the Federal Emergency Management Agency about damage levels.

It's the paradox of the city's recovery. So much has been done. And so little. So many people have, against the odds, returned. But many more never will. We've moved on with our lives. But we're still stuck.

Even a cursory trek around town reveals these contradictions: The blocks in Gentilly or eastern New Orleans where newly rebuilt homes border flood-ravaged, gutted ones; the sides of homes where fresh blooms only partially cover FEMA [Federal Emergency Management Agency] markings made in the days after the flood.

Some of the most haunting reminders can be found in New Orleans' empty school buildings, a number of which remain in limbo as school officials negotiate with the Federal Emergency Management Agency about damage levels. In the meantime, as the district embarks on an unprecedented rebuilding program, dozens of other schools sit largely untouched, festering.

A Squatter's Home

Drivers heading up Broad Street past Israel Augustine still see a crooked sign with lettering that reads: "School starts Aug. 18, 2005, 8:00 A.M." The district boarded up the front door, but a ratty chair placed by an open side window provided easy access to the building earlier this month.

Inside the first room, piles of garbage left by squatters—takeout containers, tall boys, sleeping bags, moldy clothes and pillows—coated every inch of the floor. Squatters also plundered the building of its riches, pulling apart appliances and ceiling tiles for the copper wiring inside. They broke into trophy containers, placing them in random spots throughout the building—like the middle of the grand auditorium's stage—shiny and jarring talismans from the past.

Yet many other features stood intact, like instructions scrawled on chalkboards, including the sample paper heading one teacher posted, or the phrase "Education is the basis of the future" written in both English and Spanish.

In the school's relatively undisturbed auditorium, the paint curled as it peeled off the wall near a cracked mirror. Dust and plaster coated rows of chairs. A tattered, fraying stage curtain hung forlornly.

The sound of dripping water echoed throughout the building, and the smell of stale food and fresh decay—from both wood and dead rodents—filled the air.

In one upstairs classroom, a squatter sat shirtless on a pillow, surrounded by a blanket, jugs of water, a bucket and takeout containers. He said he has stayed there off and on over the past two years, usually with a girlfriend. Work building and remodeling houses slowed a couple years after Katrina, making it harder to afford a safe place to stay. And without a picture ID he can't find jobs at all anymore.

The man said most of the squatters leave each other alone. One, named Marty, has lived in Israel Augustine for two years, turning a third-floor classroom into a kind of home, he said.

Haggling with FEMA

Shamus Rohn, director of UNITY's Abandoned Buildings Outreach Project, said untouched, unsecured school buildings can be found throughout the city.

Ramsey Green, the Recovery School District's chief operating officer, estimates the district has 40 empty and unused school buildings around the city.

"What . . . bothers me is you walk around them and hit all kinds of really confidential personal documents of kids, like birth certificates and Social Security cards lying out in the open."

"You see them deteriorating over time, so we will lose them if something doesn't happen soon," he added.

Ramsey Green, the Recovery School District's [RSD's] chief operating officer, estimates the district has 40 empty and unused school buildings around the city. But he says the district keeps the grounds landscaped—and tries to secure the buildings.

"Augustine is definitely one of the schools that we know gets infiltrated," he said. "Our folks are aware of it, and we do the best we can to protect it. But there are people out there who will go in whether it's boarded up or not."

Dozens of old schools will be demolished or converted to other uses, like community centers, in the coming months and years, Green said. But both processes take time, he added, and the district has to slog through negotiations with FEMA over the extent of the damage, and then go through detailed planning processes.

Several buildings are in limbo as the district haggles with FEMA over whether they meet the 50 percent damage threshold required for the agency to pay the cost of a new building.

"We are keeping up a number of these buildings because we are trying to get FEMA to agree to 51 percent damages," said RSD Superintendent Paul Vallas. "If we do that, we get full replacement cost and get the money to demolish them."

Vallas pointed out that the facilities master plan is largely financed with FEMA money, not city or state school construction programs. "To tear down a building that has been boarded up four or five times, you risk losing millions of dollars."

And money to secure the building in the meantime could go to support the children at active schools, Vallas adds. "It becomes a choice between a classroom or a building, and the classroom is going to win."

The district has demolished eight school buildings, and will demolish another 13 in the next six months. Israel Augustine is not slated to be demolished, and the RSD will likely hand it over to the Orleans Parish School Board sometime in the next few months, Green said.

An Open Door

While it takes some effort to get into Israel Augustine, several of the main doors to Central City's "new" Orleans Parish High School Signature Centers—as a welcome sign states—are unlocked and unboarded.

The classrooms contain signs of past parties, with heaps of cigarette butts surrounded by cans of Red Bull and a shattered Heineken bottle. On some doors, visitors have scrawled human-like figures and then used them as target practice with nail guns.

One room, with a sign warning, "Do not touch Mrs. McLain's things," was particularly barren: looters smashed the ceiling tiles, pulled apart the air-conditioning unit, and yanked out the outlet to get every last bit of valuable wiring.

They left, however, dirty mounds of student papers in the library and guidance office with individual LEAP [Louisiana Educational Assessment Program] scores and report cards that showed which students, for instance, had failed world geography.

One chalkboard introduced students to the now-infamous "I CAN Learn" algebra program—the one sold by Mose Jefferson, who last week was found guilty of bribing a school board member for her help in getting the board to buy it. Another listed three emergency numbers students could call, presumably in the event that Katrina turned serious.

And one tattered sign offered the high schoolers this advice:

"Don't let the rain stop you, or even slow you down."

14

The Bush Administration Did Not Respond Appropriately to Katrina

Becky Bohrer

Becky Bohrer is a writer for the Associated Press.

While in office, President George W. Bush defended his administration's response to Hurricane Katrina, but residents of New Orleans and Louisiana believe that his response was inadequate and slow. They believe that Bush failed to live up to his responsibility to help those recovering from the disaster, stating that federal help was slow in coming and did not do enough. Although Bush and fellow Republicans note how much money has been pumped into New Orleans, local officials and citizens believe that Bush has reneged on his promise to rebuild the city.

President George W. Bush can defend the federal government's response to Hurricane Katrina. But to Gertrude LeBlanc, the view from her home in the city's Lower Ninth Ward is all the evidence she needs to believe it was a failure.

A row of concrete foundations is all that's left where her neighbors' houses once stood.

"Bush didn't give a damn what we got," said the 73-year-old, who says she rebuilt her bright yellow house with the neat yard with help from a church group and the "little bit" in federal aid she got from the state-run program meant to help hurricane-affected homeowners, Road Home.

"To me, black folks weren't handled right, but we can't worry about it. We have to do the best we can."

Katrina's Scars Remain

When Bush leaves office next week [January 2009], New Orleans will still show the scars of Hurricane Katrina, which slammed ashore on Aug. 29, 2005. LeBlanc's neighborhood is still largely uninhabited, with weeds tall around some decrepit houses and roads cracked and warped. In some neighborhoods, apartment buildings and businesses are empty. Some houses still bear the haunting markings left by search teams in the frantic aftermath of the storm.

Bush, in some of his last comments before leaving office, said Monday at a news conference that he stood behind the federal government's response to Katrina, even though he admitted once again that some things could have been done differently and acknowledged there's still more work to do. Those words stung for people still living in the aftermath of the storm, still waiting for neighbors to come home.

President Bush is totally wrong about the federal response. . . . It was absolutely too slow in those early, critical days.

"More people need to have their own home there," Bush said. "But the systems are in place to continue the reconstruction in New Orleans. You know, people said, 'Well, the federal response was slow.' Don't tell me the federal response was slow when there was 30,000 people pulled off roofs right after the storm passed."

Bush Failed His Responsibility

The comment drew an at-times exasperated response from residents like LeBlanc and government leaders, some of whom believe federal bureaucracy is still choking recovery efforts.

"Clearly there were mistakes made at every level of government, and I and other Louisiana leaders have accepted responsibility for our own," Sen. Mary Landrieu said. "But no state is equipped to respond to a catastrophe of this magnitude, and for this reason, federal law specifically tasks the federal government to step up. It did not, and the president's failure to account for that responsibility more than three years later is terribly disappointing."

Former Gov. Kathleen Blanco, the Democrat in office when the storm hit, said state and local officials and volunteers played a major role in the rescue effort.

"President Bush is totally wrong about the federal response," said Blanco, who didn't seek reelection after her image was battered following the state's response to both hurricanes Katrina and Rita. "It was absolutely too slow in those early, critical days."

Residents here have levied criticism at every level of government since the storm, not just the White House. After levees failed during Katrina, an estimated 80 percent of New Orleans was under water. The surrounding area and parts of the Mississippi Gulf Coast were essentially wiped out. A massive military presence didn't arrive until days after the storm, and the storm is blamed in the death of more than 1,600 people across Louisiana and Mississippi.

A Governmental Tug-of-War

A tug-of-war between federal, state and local government has persisted in the years since. State and local officials have complained about red tape tied to aid programs, and Republican Gov. Bobby Jindal said Monday that a backlog of infrastructure project worksheets under appeal or in dispute with the Federal Emergency Management Agency "continues to hinder the recovery efforts of our communities that cannot finish rebuilding their schools and police and fire stations."

Residents who've returned have dealt with red tape, too, and in New Orleans, there are also issues of crime and a still-rebuilding health care system.

Since the 2005 hurricanes, the Bush administration said the federal government has set aside more than $126 billion for rebuilding and recovery. And progress is being made, including in rebuilding the levee system that protects New Orleans.

The federal government "has been a good partner in the Hurricane Katrina recovery effort, and we appreciate the efforts of both the Bush administration and the Congress in the wake of the worst natural disaster in America's history," Mississippi Gov. Haley Barbour, a Republican, said.

Bush's hurricane recovery chief, retired Maj. Gen. Doug O'Dell, said last month he believed the federal government had provided ample resources to Louisiana and Mississippi to do the needed work, and the signs of those resources are showing now.

Bush's Katrina Response Was a National Disgrace

But some still aren't convinced. "It's getting to the point it's almost like a forgotten cause," said the Rev. Terrence Ranson, who believes Bush hasn't lived up to the promises of a rebuilding he made during a speech from empty Jackson Square weeks after Katrina.

Melanie Ehrlich, a resident and frequent critic of the state-run Road Home program, said that residents, not government at any level, have rebuilt the city.

"They've done this in spite of a response by the federal government that has been too slow and much more concerned about bureaucratic rules that did not fit with this historic disaster," she said.

The Katrina response "is still a national disgrace, and New Orleans, in many places, still looks like a war-torn city."

15

The Bush Administration Provided Significant Support to the Gulf Coast

Office of the White House Press Secretary

The Office of the White House Press Secretary is responsible for releasing all official White House news.

The population of New Orleans has grown dramatically since Hurricane Katrina, due to repairs and rebuilding made possible by the federal government under the George W. Bush administration. The president's administration has played a major role in rebuilding infrastructure, supporting economic development, and restoring education in the Gulf Coast region. In addition, the Department of Justice, under President Bush's leadership, has provided forces and funding to keep New Orleans safe. Finally, President Bush successfully mobilized faith-based communities and individual Americans to come to the aid of the Gulf Coast.

Today [August 20, 2008], President [George W.] Bush visited New Orleans, Louisiana, and the Mississippi Gulf Coast to discuss the major improvements taking place in the Gulf Coast region over the past three years. August 29, 2008, marks the three-year anniversary of Hurricane Katrina's landfall along the Gulf Coast of the United States. President and Mrs. [Laura] Bush continue to provide substantial support to the local citizens and leaders who are rebuilding their homes, lives, and communities in the wake of Hurricanes Katrina and

"Fact Sheet: Rebuilding the Gulf Coast," The White House, Office of the Press Secretary, August 20, 2008.

Rita. Significant progress has been made in the region, and the federal government has pledged to remain a steadfast, supportive partner for the local leaders who must continue to drive this rebuilding effort.

New Orleans Has Grown

- The population of the Greater New Orleans metro area is up to 87 percent of pre-Katrina estimates.

- Greater New Orleans added 8,600 jobs in the past year.

- New Orleans' 2007 visitor numbers increased from 3.7 million in 2006 to 7.1 million in 2007. In 2007, visitors spent a total of $4.8 billion, compared to $2.8 billion in 2006.

- There are more restaurants open for business today in New Orleans than were open before Katrina.

[Federal] funds are helping more than 115,000 home-owners in disaster-affected areas repair and rebuild their homes, while also providing for vital economic and community development projects and the building of affordable rental and mixed-income housing.

Federal Aid to the Gulf Coast

The federal government has provided more than $126 billion—$140 billion including tax relief—to the Gulf Coast region. This funding is helping fulfill vital needs, including housing reconstruction, rental assistance, infrastructure repair, flood insurance payments, education, health care, criminal justice, and debris removal.

- Of this funding, $101 billion—81 percent—has either been disbursed or is available for states to draw from.

President Bush and his administration are working with state and local leaders to help them rebuild the region and support vital reforms that will create stronger, more hopeful communities.

Under the president's leadership, Congress has provided more than $20 billion in federal funds through the U.S. Department of Housing and Urban Development's (HUD) Community Development Block Grant program (including $13.4 billion for Louisiana and $5.5 billion for Mississippi) to rebuild damaged housing and other infrastructure. These funds are helping more than 115,000 homeowners in disaster-affected areas repair and rebuild their homes, while also providing for vital economic and community development projects and the building of affordable rental and mixed-income housing. This is the largest housing recovery program in U.S. history.

The Bush White House Supported Levee Repair

With the president's leadership, the federal government has appropriated a total of $12.85 billion since 2005 to repair and strengthen the levees. On June 30, 2008, President Bush signed the 2008 Supplemental Appropriations Act, which allocated an additional $5.8 billion for completing levee improvements in metro New Orleans. Prior supplemental appropriations for New Orleans hurricane protection totaled $7.04 billion. On August 7, 2008, President Bush allowed Louisiana to pay its share of the levee reconstruction over 30 years—ensuring that the state will not have to choose between rebuilding flood walls and its other vital recovery projects.

- The U.S. Army Corps of Engineers (Corps) completed the repair and restoration of 220 miles of flood walls and levees in June 2006. The Corps continues to improve the hurricane protection system, and the New

Orleans area now has the best flood protection in its history. In April 2008, the Corps awarded its largest design-build contract ever, and is currently on track to meet its goal of completing 100-year protection by the year 2011.

- In December 2006, President Bush signed legislation allowing Louisiana to share in revenues from drilling along the Outer Continental Shelf (OCS)—realizing an objective that the state of Louisiana has pursued for 60 years. The people of Louisiana passed a constitutional amendment dedicating those funds to hurricane protection and restoration of coastal wetlands. OCS revenue will begin flowing to the state in 2010 and is expected to reach $600 million to $800 million per year by 2017.

The Bush Administration Is Strengthening Infrastructure

- The Federal Emergency Management Agency (FEMA) will provide more than $12.1 billion to repair and replace damaged public infrastructure such as schools, firehouses, water systems, public buildings, and public utilities, as well as to fund emergency protective measures and debris removal. $11 billion already has been made available to the states.

- The U.S. Department of Transportation will provide a total of $3.5 billion for roads, bridges, aviation facilities, and other transportation projects in the Gulf [region].

- The Office of the Federal Coordinator [for Gulf Coast Rebuilding], through a partnership with other federal, state, and local leaders, convened a series of "workout sessions" to drive key public infrastructure projects toward completion.

- Since Hurricane Katrina, FEMA has funded the removal of 111 million cubic yards of debris in Alabama, Louisiana, and Mississippi.

President Bush and Congress have provided $13.8 billion in tax incentives and relief for hurricane victims and small businesses.

President Bush Supports Economic Development

- The U.S. Small Business Administration disbursed nearly $6.5 billion in low-cost disaster loans to home-owners, renters, and business owners in the Gulf Coast states affected by the hurricanes. In Louisiana, more than 71,000 disaster loans have been approved and $4.2 billion disbursed. In Mississippi, more than 27,000 disaster loans have been approved and $1.4 billion disbursed.

- The U.S. Department of Labor awarded more than $418 million in grants to support the creation of temporary jobs, provide impacted workers with education and training for new career opportunities, and help local leaders across the Gulf Coast build and improve integrated systems of workforce development.

- President Bush and his administration initiated the Gulf Coast Workforce Development Initiative. As of the end of May 2008, the initiative had trained 18,768 individuals and another 2,036 are currently enrolled in training programs.

- President Bush and Congress have provided $13.8 billion in tax incentives and relief for hurricane victims and small businesses through the Katrina Emergency Tax Relief Act and the Gulf Opportunity Zone Act.

- Ninety-nine percent of all claims through FEMA's National Flood Insurance Program (NFIP), which help affected policyholders rebuild or relocate, have been closed. Under this program, $13.5 billion has been provided to Louisiana and $2.47 billion has been provided to Mississippi.

- The U.S. Department of Agriculture has distributed $250 million to help farmers affected by the storms.

President Bush Helps Schools and Hospitals

The U.S. Department of Education has provided almost $2 billion in grant assistance to reopen schools in the Gulf Coast region and to help educate students displaced by the storms. Affected colleges and universities received more than $300 million, and another $30 million has been used to help recruit and retain educators along the Gulf Coast. The department also directed almost $400 million in loans to historically black colleges and universities affected by the storms.

The Laura Bush Foundation for America's Libraries has awarded competitive grants to 78 elementary and high schools to buy books for hurricane-affected school libraries in the Gulf Coast region, totaling more than $3.7 million.

- The U.S. Department of Education has supported city and state leaders in transforming the public education system in New Orleans. The department has invested more than $45 million in strengthening a growing number of charter schools, which has given educators more flexibility, required greater accountability, and provided parents with more choices for their children.

FEMA provided more than $2.3 billion to Louisiana and more than $347 million to Mississippi to restore school buildings. Today, there are 85 public schools open in New Orleans to serve a projected 33,000 students, more than enough seats for all children.

Since Hurricane Katrina, Mrs. Bush has visited numerous schools and saluted community leaders in more than 20 trips to the Gulf Coast region. Through its Gulf Coast School Library Recovery Initiative, the Laura Bush Foundation for America's Libraries has awarded competitive grants to 78 elementary and high schools to buy books for hurricane-affected school libraries in the Gulf Coast region, totaling more than $3.7 million.

The U.S. Department of Health and Human Services (HHS) has promoted a more efficient, effective and compassionate health care system. It provided approximately $2.7 billion for health care and social services. This includes approximately $1.3 billion in Louisiana alone to provide health care services for low-income and uninsured mental health services, social services, support for primary care clinics and private hospitals, and recruitment and retention incentives for doctors, nurses, and other health professionals in New Orleans. HHS is also working closely with the state of Louisiana to implement comprehensive reforms that will improve health care quality and increase citizens' access to high-quality health care, regardless of income.

The U.S. Department of Justice Protects New Orleans

The U.S. Department of Justice (DOJ) provided more than $86 million to the state of Louisiana to restore criminal justice infrastructure and better equip local law enforcement agencies. These funds have provided local police and sheriffs with vital equipment; helped reestablish local court operations; helped pay the salaries of prosecutors and investigators; and supported programs that help prevent youth violence and other risky behavior.

- DOJ created the Hurricane Katrina Fraud Task Force to deter, investigate, and prosecute disaster-related federal crimes—892 prosecutions to date. In August 2007, New Orleans installed its first Inspector General with full support of the federal government. The Federal Coordinator hosted a meeting of key federal Inspectors General in May 2008 and a follow-up meeting last month, where a pledge of continued cooperation was made by more than 30 federal, state, and local leaders.

- DOJ has also played a lead role in the Southeast Louisiana Criminal Justice Recovery Task Force, a coalition of local, state, and federal criminal justice leaders working to restore vital infrastructure and establish a more effective justice system. The task force is helping to train New Orleans police officers, sharing intelligence between the FBI and local law enforcement, exploring ways to better harmonize efforts such as the establishment of a regional crime lab and regional training academy, and working to improve interoperability between state police and local law enforcement.

President Bush Mobilizes Americans to Help

- This administration has increased to unprecedented levels the federal support of the Gulf Coast's faith-based and community nonprofits that serve as frontline allies in the rebuilding effort. In 2006 alone, the federal government awarded more than 2,100 direct, competitive grants to faith-based and other nonprofit organizations in Gulf Coast states totaling more than $1.8 billion. Of these funds, nearly $200 million has been awarded to Louisiana's faith-based and nonprofit organizations.

- Following the storms, the nation's armies of compassion responded to the president's call for aid by volunteering at historic levels. Americans have donated more than $3.5 billion to help the recovery and rebuilding effort. More than 93,000 participants in national service programs have given more than 3.5 million hours of service in response to the devastation inflicted by Katrina. National service participants from AmeriCorps and Senior Corps have supported and managed more than 262,000 community volunteers.

16

Global Warming Will Produce More Katrina-Like Storms

Joseph Romm

Joseph Romm is a senior fellow at the Center for American Progress and the author of Hell or High Water.

Global warming will likely produce storms larger and more intense than Hurricane Katrina. Some storms may become immense as global warming increases the temperature of the oceans. It is possible that category 6 super storms could become common, and that the hurricane season could last longer than at present. The climatic conditions created by global warming are also likely to make such storms more dangerous at landfall. The only way to prevent such monster storms from forming is to reduce carbon emissions immediately.

Hurricane season officially begins June 1—though global warming will ultimately move that date up just as it is moving up the spring snowmelt. Indeed, some evidence suggests the hurricane season has been getting longer for decades.

As Jeff Masters, our favorite meteorologist and hurricane blogger, noted in November [2008], "This year is now the only hurricane season on record in the Atlantic that has featured major hurricanes in five separate months." . . . Saturday, Masters explained that had "the large extratropical storm (90L) that has been pounding Florida" this week "spent another six hours over water, it very likely would have been declared a

Joseph Romm, "Why Global Warming Means Killer Storms Worse than Katrina and Gustav, Part 1," *Climate Progress*, May 25, 2009. Copyright © 2009 ClimateProgress.org Cimate Progress (CAP) Action. Reproduced by permission.

tropical/subtropical depression/storm"—that is, it would have been "the season's first named storm." So I won't wait until June 1 to revise and update some posts from last year on why global warming will lead to much worse killer storms.

Hurricanes Can Become Immense

Hurricanes can get much, much bigger and stronger than we have so far seen in the Atlantic. The most intense Pacific storm on record was Super Typhoon Tip in 1979, which reached maximum sustained winds of 190 mph near the center. On its wide rim, gale force winds (39 mph) extended over a diameter of an astonishing 1,350 miles. It would have covered nearly half the continental United States.

> *Global warming heats both the sea surface and the deep water, thus creating ideal conditions for a hurricane to survive and thrive in its long journey from tropical depression to Category 4 or 5 super storm.*

"More than half the total hurricane damage in the United States (normalized for inflation and population trends) was caused by just five events," explained MIT [Massachusetts Institute of Technology] hurricane expert Kerry Emanuel in an e-mail. Storms that are Category 4 and 5 at landfall (or just before) are what destroy major cities like New Orleans and Galveston with devastating winds, rains, and storm surges. . . .

The National Climatic Data Center 2006 report on Katrina begins its explanation by noting that the [sea] surface temperatures (SSTs) in the Gulf of Mexico during the last week in August 2005 "were one to two degrees Celsius above normal, and the warm temperatures extended to a considerable depth through the upper ocean layer." The report continues, "Also, Katrina crossed the 'loop current' (belt of even warmer water), during which time explosive intensification occurred. The temperature of the ocean surface is a critical element in the formation and strength of hurricanes."

An important factor was that the ocean warming had penetrated to a considerable depth. One of the ways that hurricanes are weakened is the upwelling of colder, deeper water due to the hurricane's own violent action. But if the deeper water is also warm, it doesn't weaken the hurricane. In fact, it may continue to intensify. Global warming heats both the sea surface and the deep water, thus creating ideal conditions for a hurricane to survive and thrive in its long journey from tropical depression to Category 4 or 5 super storm.

Warming Oceans

A 2005 study, "Penetration of Human-Induced Warming into the World's Oceans," led by Scripps Institution of Oceanography compared actual ocean temperature data from the surface down to hundreds of meters (in the Atlantic, Pacific, and Indian oceans) with climate models and concluded:

> A warming signal has penetrated into the world's oceans over the past 40 years. The signal is complex, with a vertical structure that varies widely by ocean; it cannot be explained by natural internal climate variability or solar and volcanic forcing, but is well simulated by two anthropogenically forced climate models. We conclude that it is of human origin, a conclusion robust to observational sampling and model differences. . . .

And yes, the latest analysis shows "that ocean heat content has indeed been increasing in recent decades, just like the models said it should." . . .

The Formation of Tropical Cyclones

Tropical cyclones are threshold events—if sea surface temperatures are below 80°F (26.5°C), they do not form. Some analysis even suggests there is a sea surface temperature "threshold [close to 83°F] necessary for the development of major hurricanes." Global warming may actually cause some hurricanes and some major hurricanes to develop that otherwise would not have (by raising sea surface temperatures above the necessary threshold at the right place or time).

And the more warm, deep water that gets generated by global warming, the more super-intense hurricanes we will see. No wonder ABC News reported in 2006 that hurricane scientists are considering adding a Category 6, for hurricanes above 175 miles per hour. Ultimately, they may become common.

If we don't reverse our emissions paths quickly, global temperatures will rise faster and faster through 2100 and beyond. This will translate into warmer oceans in all three dimensions: Warmth will spread over wider swaths of the ocean as well as deeper below the surface—we've already seen that in the first known tropical cyclone in the South Atlantic (2004) and the first known tropical cyclone to strike Spain (2005). That means we will probably see stronger hurricanes farther north along the East Coast in the coming decades.

If a storm taking the same track as Gustav (or Katrina) occurred in 2050, then, rather than weakening before making landfall, it would probably have strengthened considerably, creating far more havoc.

Expanded Hurricane Season

More intense storms will be seen earlier and later in the season. The 2005 hurricane season was the most striking example of that trend, with Emily the earliest-forming Category 5 hurricane on record in the Atlantic, in July, and Zeta, the longest-lived tropical cyclone to form in December and cross over into the next year, where it became the longest-lived January tropical cyclone.

We have already seen a statistically significant increase in the length of the average hurricane season over the last several decades, according to a recent analysis. The data from the past century indicates that a 1°F increase in sea surface temperatures leads to an extra five tropical storms a year in the Atlantic—an ominous statistic in a world taking no actions to stop a projected 3°F increase in average sea surface temperatures over the Atlantic hurricane-forming region by 2050, and more than double that by century's end. . . .

Katrina and Gustav

My key point here is one that is rarely discussed in the literature dealing with global warming and hurricanes: All things being equal, if a storm taking the same track of Gustav (or Katrina) occurred in 2050, then, rather than weakening before making landfall, it would probably have strengthened considerably, creating far more havoc.

Let's look at the region in 2050, assuming BAU (business as usual) warming, or no effort to reverse current emissions trends. . . .

Now that is bad news for New Orleans, the Gulf Coast, and the South Atlantic. The average warming in the Gulf, Caribbean, and coastal Atlantic is 1°C to 2°C, but this model has an enormous body of very warm water 2°C to 3°C over much of the typical storm path for a hurricane like Katrina or Gustav. There are two relevant points to recall:

1. The National Climatic Data Center 2006 report on Katrina notes that the sea surface temperatures (SSTs) in the Gulf of Mexico during the last week in August 2005 "were one to two degrees Celsius above normal."

2. In the case of both Katrina and Gustav, they hit colder water before hitting the coast—a key reason they were far weaker at landfall than they might have been, . . .

Now imagine we are in the year 2050 with the same storm track. We could easily be talking a Gustav 2050 that is a Category 4 or even Category 5 at landfall, rather than just a strong Category 2.

What about Katrina? It did reach Category 5 status in the Gulf, but it made landfall only as a Category 3. . . . Again, cold water played a role. . . .

Obviously, Katrina was able to ride the Gulf Loop Current and Eddy Vortex closer to the coast than Gustav, but it still smashed into cold water. Again, in 2050, that weakening is going to be a lot less likely to occur.

Hurricanes and the Gulf Stream

What precisely would happen if a hurricane was ever able to ride warm Gulf water all the way to landfall? We have some idea because that appears to have happened once in the relatively recent past:

> An example of how deep warm water, including the Loop Current, can allow a hurricane to strengthen, if other conditions are also favorable, is Hurricane Camille, which made landfall on the Mississippi Gulf Coast in August of 1969. Camille formed in the deep warm waters of the Caribbean, which enabled it to rapidly intensify into a Category 3 hurricane in one day. It rounded the western tip of Cuba, and its path took it directly over the Loop Current, all the way north toward the coast, during which time the rapid intensification continued. Camille became a Category 5 hurricane, with an intensity rarely seen, and extremely high winds that were maintained until landfall (190 mph/305 km/h sustained winds were estimated to have occurred in a very small area to the right of the eye).

That of course was pure happenstance, pure bad luck. But by mid-century, the whole Gulf in the summer is going to be much, much warmer, thanks not to bad luck but to human emissions. So it seems a near certainty that the Gulf Coast will see one or more Category 5s make landfall in the coming decades. . . .

Only one major issue remains, I think. Clearly global warming means warmer surface water and . . . warmer deep water. All things being equal, that means future hurricanes that travel the same path are going to stay stronger longer and possibly even intensify where earlier hurricanes had weakened.

If we don't reverse emissions trends soon, then Category 4 and 5 storms smashing into the Gulf Coast seem likely to become rather common in the second half of this century.

Emission Trends Must Be Reversed

What we don't know is if, in fact, all things will be equal. Perhaps global warming will create other conditions that might serve to weaken hurricanes or change their storm path. Some have suggested that climate change could lead to a permanent El Niño condition. That would be an unmitigated catastrophe for the planet, but would probably lead to fewer Atlantic hurricanes. Global warming could also lead to more wind shear, which tends to break up hurricanes.

That said, serious global warming has been going on for a few decades now, and just this decade we've had two major hurricanes ride straight up into the New Orleans area, three if you count Rita. So I don't think it makes much sense to hope or expect that future global warming means significantly fewer major hurricanes that end up on a path toward the Louisiana coast.

We are stuck with a fair amount of warming over the next few decades no matter what we do. But if we don't reverse emissions trends soon, then Category 4 and 5 storms smashing into the Gulf Coast seem likely to become rather common in the second half of this century. And that will be a doubly untenable situation because by then we will be probably also be facing sea level rise of a few inches a decade or more.

Preserving the habitability of the Gulf and South Atlantic coasts post-2050 can only occur if we reverse U.S. and global emissions trends immediately.

17

Global Warming May Not Produce More Katrina-Like Storms

Eric Berger

Eric Berger is a science writer and blogger for the Houston Chronicle.

Although most scientists believe that global warming will increase hurricane intensity and frequency, a new study by Kerry Emanuel of the Massachusetts Institute of Technology reveals that may not be the case. Emanuel used a new technique of computer modeling to try to project two hundred years into the future. To his surprise, he discovered that his models show a drop in the number of storms. It is possible, however, that although there will be fewer storms, they may increase in intensity. Emanuel's study, however, emphasizes that there is considerable uncertainty in predicting such events.

One of the most influential scientists behind the theory that global warming has intensified recent hurricane activity says he will reconsider his stand.

Hurricane Frequency May Not Increase with Global Warming

The hurricane expert, Kerry Emanuel of the Massachusetts Institute of Technology, unveiled a novel technique for predicting future hurricane activity this week [April 2008]. The new

Eric Berger, "Hurricane Expert Reconsiders Global Warming's Impact," *Houston Chronicle*, April 12, 2008. Copyright © 2008 Houston Chronicle Publishing Company Division. Republished with permission of Houston Chronicle, conveyed through Copyright Clearance Center, Inc.

work suggests that, even in a dramatically warming world, hurricane frequency and intensity may not substantially rise during the next two centuries.

The research, appearing in the March issue of *Bulletin of the American Meteorological Society,* is all the more remarkable coming from Emanuel, a highly visible leader in his field and long an ardent proponent of a link between global warming and much stronger hurricanes.

His changing views could influence other scientists.

"The results surprised me," Emanuel said of his work, adding that global warming may still play a role in raising the intensity of hurricanes. What that role is, however, remains far from certain.

Emanuel's work uses a new method of computer modeling that did a reasonable job of simulating past hurricane fluctuations. He, therefore, believes the models may have predictive value for future activity.

The new work suggests that, even in a dramatically warming world, hurricane frequency and intensity may not substantially rise during the next two centuries.

During and after the 2004 and 2005 hurricane seasons, which were replete with mega-storms and U.S. landfalls, scientists dived into the question of whether rising ocean temperatures, attributed primarily to global warming, were causing stronger storms.

Among the first to publish was Emanuel, who—just three weeks before Hurricane Katrina's landfall—published a paper in *Nature* that concluded a key measurement of the power dissipated by a storm during its lifetime had risen dramatically since the mid-1970s.

In the future, he argued, incredibly active hurricane years such as 2005 would become the norm rather than flukes.

Hurricane Science Remains Uncertain

This view, amplified by environmentalists and others concerned about global warming, helped establish in the public's mind that "super" hurricanes were one of climate change's most critical threats. A satellite image of a hurricane emanating from a smokestack featured prominently in promotions for Al Gore's *An Inconvenient Truth*.

"Kerry had the good fortune, or maybe the bad fortune, to publish when the world's attention was focused on hurricanes in 2005," Roger Pielke Jr., who studies science and policy at the University of Colorado, said of Emanuel. "Kerry's work was seized upon in the debate."

After the 2005 hurricane season, a series of other papers were published that appeared to show, among other things, that the most intense hurricanes were becoming more frequent.

What has not been as broadly disseminated, say Pielke and some hurricane scientists, is that other research papers have emerged that suggest global warming has yet to leave an imprint on hurricane activity. One of them, published late last year in *Nature*, found that warming seas may not increase hurricane intensity.

That paper's coauthor, Gabriel Vecchi, a research scientist with the National Oceanic and Atmospheric Administration, said Emanuel's new work highlights the great uncertainty that remains in hurricane science.

"While his results don't rule out the possibility that global warming has contributed to the recent increase in activity in the Atlantic, they suggest that other factors—possibly in addition to global warming—are likely to have been substantial contributors to the observed increase in activity," Vecchi said.

Scientists wrangling with the hurricane–global warming question have faced two primary difficulties. The first is that the hurricane record before 1970 is not entirely reliable, making it nearly impossible to assess with precision whether hurricane activity has increased during the last century.

The second problem comes through the use of computer models to predict hurricane activity. Most climate models, which simulate global atmospheric conditions for centuries to come, cannot detect individual tropical systems.

Emanuel's new research attempts to get around that by inserting "seeds" of tropical systems throughout the climate models and seeing which develop into tropical storms and hurricanes. The "seeds," bits of computer code, tend to develop when simulated atmospheric conditions, such as low wind shear, are ripe for hurricane formation.

Models Offer Mixed Messages

In the new paper, Emanuel and his coauthors project activity nearly two centuries hence, finding an overall drop in the number of hurricanes around the world, while the intensity of storms in some regions does rise.

For example, with Atlantic hurricanes, two of the seven model simulations Emanuel ran suggested that the overall intensity of storms would decline. Five models suggested a modest increase.

"The take-home message is that we've got a lot of work to do," Emanuel said. "There's still a lot of uncertainty in this problem. The bulk of the evidence is that hurricane power will go up, but in some places it will go down."

The issue probably will not be resolved until better computer models are developed, said Judith Curry, of the Georgia Institute of Technology, a leading hurricane and climate scholar.

By publishing his new paper, and by the virtue of his high profile, Emanuel could be a catalyst for further agreement in the field of hurricanes and global warming, Curry said.

The generally emerging view, she said, seems to be that global warming may cause some increase in intensity, that this increase will develop slowly over time, and that it likely will lead to a few more Category 4 and Category 5 storms. How many? When? No one yet knows.

Organizations to Contact

The editors have compiled the following list of organizations concerned with the issues debated in this book. The descriptions are derived from materials provided by the organizations. All have publications or information available for interested readers. The list was compiled on the date of publication of the present volume; names, addresses, phone and fax numbers, and e-mail and Internet addresses may change. Be aware that many organizations take several weeks or longer to respond to inquiries, so allow as much time as possible.

American Red Cross
National Headquarters, 2025 E Street NW
Washington, DC   20006
(202) 303-5000
Web site: www.redcross.org

The American Red Cross is the United States' oldest and largest emergency response organization. Its goal is to prevent and mitigate human suffering caused by emergencies such as Hurricane Katrina. The American Red Cross Web site includes many publications about disaster preparedness as well as archival materials concerning Hurricane Katrina. Of special note is the photo library, available through the Web site, including high-quality photographs with captions.

Federal Emergency Management Agency (FEMA)
500 C Street SW, Washington, DC   20472
(800) 621-3362 • fax: (800) 827-8112
e-mail: AskFEMA@dhs.gov
Web site: www.fema.gov

The Federal Emergency Management Agency (FEMA) is a division of the Office of Homeland Security charged with responding to and managing relief during any natural or man-made disaster in the United States. FEMA's Web site includes information about various kinds of disasters and about the processes for responding to disasters. A large section of the Web site is devoted to providing information and resources about hurricanes. In addition, FEMA maintains a large archive of information concerning Hurricane Katrina and the federal response to the disaster.

National Aeronautics and Space Administration (NASA)

300 E Street SW, Washington, DC   20546-0001
(202) 358-0001 • fax: (202) 358-4338
Web site: www.nasa.gov

In addition to the National Aeronautics and Space Administration's (NASA's) mission to lead the way in space exploration, scientific discovery, and aeronautics research, the agency also provides a large section on Hurricane Katrina, through its Hurricane/Tropical Cyclones resource page and archives. Articles such as "A NASA Look Back at Hurricane Katrina" and "Hurricane Katrina: Natural Hazards" provide important information about the storm and its aftermath. Of special interest are the "NASA Post-Hurricane Katrina Images Available on Google Earth" and "Hurricane Katrina Arrives: Images of the Day," which offer striking visual images of the disaster.

National Hurricane Center (NHC)

11691 Seventeenth Street SW, Miami, FL   33165-2149
e-mail: nhc.public.affairs@noaa.com
Web site: www.nhc.noaa.gov

The National Hurricane Center (NHC) is a division of the National Weather Service specifically charged with researching and predicting hurricanes and other tropical weather. The NHC Web site provides a wealth of publications, including hurricane and natural disaster brochures. In addition, the NHC provides downloadable hurricane tracking charts. Especially useful for the study of Hurricane Katrina is the section of the Web site devoted to storm archives.

National Institute of Environmental Health Sciences (NIEHS)

PO Box 12233, MD K3-16
Research Triangle Park, NC   27709-2233
(919) 541-3345 • fax: (919) 541-4395
Web site: www.niehs.nih.gov

The mission of the National Institute of Environmental Health Sciences (NIEHS) is to reduce the burden of human illness and disability by understanding how the environment influences the development and progression of human disease. Of special note is the section of the NIEHS Web site that concerns the response to Hurricane Katrina. The NIEHS portal offers users access to demographic information, public health data, and environmental data. This information is particularly useful for those studying the environmental impact of both the hurricane and the response to the hurricane.

New Orleans Redevelopment Authority (NORA)

1340 Poydras Street, Suite 600, New Orleans, Louisiana   70112
(504) 658-4400 • fax: (504) 658-4551
e-mail: nora@cityofno.com
Web site: www.noraworks.org

The New Orleans Redevelopment Authority (NORA) works to renovate and remove slums and blight from the city of New Orleans through the acquisition of properties and support for neighborhood development. The organization's Web site describes all programs currently being undertaken in New Orleans as well as providing useful links to other resources and organizations. Publications include policy guides and frequently asked questions.

OneStorm

600 First Avenue N, Suite 307, St. Petersburg, FL   33701
fax: (727) 381-9462
Web site: www.onestorm.org

OneStorm is a company dedicated to providing free hurricane preparedness resources for families. The Web site includes over two hundred hurricane preparedness, response, and recovery articles designed to help educate the public. In addition, the Web site also allows users to develop a personalized hurricane preparedness plan through an easy-to-use, interactive program. This also includes downloadable forms such as shopping lists and contact cards.

U.S. Army Corps of Engineers

441 G Street NW, Washington, DC   20314-1000
(202) 761-0011
e-mail: hq-publicaffairs@usace.army.mil
Web site: www.usace.army.mil

The U.S. Army Corps of Engineers provides vital public engineering services in peace and war to strengthen American security, energize the economy, and reduce risks from disaster. The corps works to deliver sustainable solutions for engineering challenges, such as making the Gulf Coast safe from hurricanes. The corps offers a number of documents, pamphlets, and fact sheets such as *Greater New Orleans Hurricane and Storm Damage Risk Reduction System: Facts and Figures*. The corps also maintains a large archive of material specifically related to Hurricane Katrina.

Bibliography

Books

Jenni Bergal et al. *City Adrift: New Orleans Before and After Katrina*. Baton Rouge: Louisiana State University Press, 2007.

Douglas Brinkley *The Great Deluge: Hurricane Katrina, New Orleans, and the Mississippi Gulf Coast*. New York: Morrow, 2006.

Christopher Cooper and Robert Block *Disaster: Hurricane Katrina and the Failure of Homeland Security*. New York: Times Books, 2006.

Michael Eric Dyson *Come Hell or High Water: Hurricane Katrina and the Color of Disaster*. New York: Basic Civitas, 2006.

Chester Hartman and Gregory D. Squires, eds. *There Is No Such Thing as a Natural Disaster: Race, Class, and Hurricane Katrina*. New York: Routledge, 2006.

Jed Horne *Breach of Faith: Hurricane Katrina and the Near Death of a Great American City*. New York: Random House, 2006.

John McQuaid and Mark Schleifstein *Path of Destruction: The Devastation of New Orleans and the Coming Age of Superstorms*. New York: Little, Brown, and Co., 2006.

Chris Rose · *1 Dead in Attic: After Katrina*. New York: Simon & Schuster Paperbacks, 2007.

Frances Fragos Townsend · *The Federal Response to Hurricane Katrina: Lessons Learned*. Washington, DC: White House, 2006.

Joseph B. Treaster · *Hurricane Force: In the Path of America's Deadliest Storms*. Boston: Kingfisher, 2007.

David Dante Troutt, ed. · *After the Storm: Black Intellectuals Explore the Meaning of Hurricane Katrina*. New York: New Press, 2006.

Ivor van Heerden and Mike Bryan · *The Storm: What Went Wrong and Why During Hurricane Katrina: The Inside Story from One Louisiana Scientist*. New York: Viking, 2006.

Periodicals

Becky Bohrer · "Progress Celebrated on Fourth Anniversary of Hurricane Katrina," *Insurance Journal*, August 31, 2009.

Shaila Dewan · "Katrina Victims Will Not Have to Vacate Trailers," *New York Times*, June 3, 2009.

Peter Eisler · "Probe: New Orleans Flood Control Pumps Not Reliable," *USA Today*, August 25, 2009.

Sheri Fink · "Strained by Katrina, a Hospital Faced Deadly Choices," *New York Times*, August 25, 2009.

Jordan Flaherty	"Homeless and Struggling in New Orleans," *Dissident Voice*, August 25, 2009.
Tanya Lewis	"New Orleans Gets Back on Track with Comms," *PR Week*, March 23, 2009.
Amy Liu and Nigel Holmes	"The State of New Orleans: An Update," *New York Times*, August 27, 2009.
James Ridgeway	"The Secret History of Hurricane Katrina," *Mother Jones*, August 28, 2009.
Ron Schachter	"Fresh Chance for New Orleans Schools," *District Administration*, December 2006.
Rebecca Solnit	"Four Years On, Katrina Remains Cursed by Rumour, Cliche, Lies and Racism," *Guardian*, August 26, 2009.
A.C. Thompson	"Katrina's Hidden Race War," *Nation*, December 17, 2008.

Internet Resources

| Sean Alfano | "Bush Knew of Katrina's Wrath Day Prior," CBS News, March 1, 2006. www.cbsnews.com. |

Richard Bessar	"Protecting Older Adults During Public Health Emergencies," Testimony Before the Special Committee on Aging, United States Senate, June 24, 2009. http://aging.senate.gov.
Sean Crowley	"On Katrina Anniversary Week, Coalition Urges Army Corps to Honor Obama's Priority to Restore Wetlands," Environment News Service, August 26, 2009. http://world-wire.com.
Debbie Elliott	"The Gulf Coast's Recovery: Uneven and Uneasy," NPR, August 27, 2009. www.npr.org.
Sarah Jane Gilbert and Stacey M. Childress	"HBS Cases: Reforming New Orleans Schools After Katrina," Working Knowledge, Harvard Business School, July 14, 2008. http://hbswk.hbs.edu.
Sharon Hanshaw	"Four Years After Katrina, 100 Days to Copenhagen," Huffington Post, August 28, 2009. www.huffingtonpost.com.
Ausa Vickie E. Leduc	"Recipient of Hurricane Katrina Disaster Funds Sentenced for Stealing $60,200," Department of Justice, April 13, 2009. www.dhs.gov.
Jennifer Liberto	"New Orleans Economy: Recovery Interrupted," CNNMoney.com, August 20, 2009. http://money.cnn.com.

Tolu Olorunda   "Hurricane Katrina and the Aftermath of Apathy," Daily Voice, August 28, 2009. http://thedailyvoice.com.

Craig Palosky and   "Major House-to-House Survey Finds New Orleans Area Residents Hit Hard by Katrina and Struggling with Serious Life Challenges," Kaiser Family Foundation, May 10, 2007. www.kff.org.
Rakesh Singh

Index